As one of the world's longest established
and best-known travel brands,
Thomas Cook are the experts in travel.

For more than 135 years our
guidebooks have unlocked the secrets
of destinations around the world,
sharing with travellers a wealth of
experience and a passion for travel.

**Rely on Thomas Cook as your
travelling companion on your next trip
and benefit from our unique heritage.**

uides

NEAPOLITAN
RIVIERA

Your travelling companion since 1873

Thomas
Cook

Written by Ryan Levitt and updated by Jo-Ann Titmarsh

Published by Thomas Cook Publishing
A division of Thomas Cook Tour Operations Limited
Company registration no. 3772199 England
The Thomas Cook Business Park, Unit 9, Coningsby Road,
Peterborough PE3 8SB, United Kingdom
Email: books@thomascook.com, Tel: + 44 (0) 1733 416477
www.thomascookpublishing.com

Produced by Cambridge Publishing Management Limited
Burr Elm Court, Main Street, Caldecote CB23 7NU

ISBN: 978-1-84848-252-4

First edition © 2008 Thomas Cook Publishing
This second edition © 2010
Text © Thomas Cook Publishing
Maps © Thomas Cook Publishing/PCGraphics (UK) Limited

Series Editor: Adam Royal
Production/DTP: Steven Collins

Printed and bound in Spain by GraphyCems

Cover photography © Bon Appetit/Alamy

CONTENTS

INTRODUCTION 5
Getting to know the
    Neapolitan Riviera 8
The best of the
    Neapolitan Riviera 10
Symbols key 12

RESORTS 13
Naples 15
Procida.......................................22
Ischia...29
Capri 35
Sorrento....................................43
Sorrentine Peninsula:
    the north coast........................50
Positano....................................57
Praiano......................................63

EXCURSIONS 67
Rome 69
Herculaneum & Vesuvius 74
Pompeii.....................................78
Amalfi..82
Salerno......................................85

LIFESTYLE 87
Food & drink..............................88
Menu decoder 92
Shopping...................................95
Children 99
Sports & activities....................102
Festivals & events 104

PRACTICAL INFORMATION 107
Accommodation 108
Preparing to go 110
During your stay 114

INDEX................................125

MAPS
Neapolitan Riviera.......................6
Naples 14
Ischia...28
Capri 34
Sorrento....................................44
Positano....................................56
Rome 68

WHAT'S IN YOUR GUIDEBOOK?

Independent authors Impartial, up-to-date information from our travel experts who meticulously source local knowledge.

Experience Thomas Cook's 165 years in the travel industry and guidebook publishing enriches every word with expertise you can trust.

Travel know-how Thomas Cook has thousands of staff working around the globe, all living and breathing travel.

Editors Travel-publishing professionals, pulling everything together to craft a perfect blend of words, pictures, maps and design.

You, the traveller We deliver a practical, no-nonsense approach to information, geared to how you really use it.

▶ *The city of Naples*

 # INTRODUCTION
Getting to know the Neapolitan Riviera

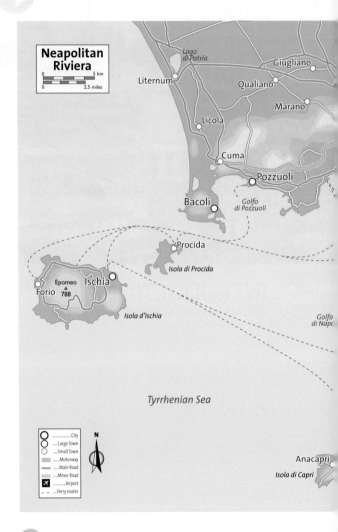

Neapolitan Riviera

| 0 | | | 5 km |
| 0 | | 2.5 miles | |

Lago di Patria

Giugliano

Liternum

Qualiano

Marano

Licola

Cuma

Pozzuoli

Bacoli

Golfo di Pozzuoli

Procida

Isola di Procida

Epomeo ▲ 788

Ischia

Forio

Isola d'Ischia

Golfo di Napoli

Tyrrhenian Sea

○ ....City
○ ....Large Town
○ ....Small Town
▬ ....Motorway
━━ ....Main Road
━━ ....Minor Road
✈ ....Airport
- - - ....Ferry routes

N

Anacapri

Isola di Capri

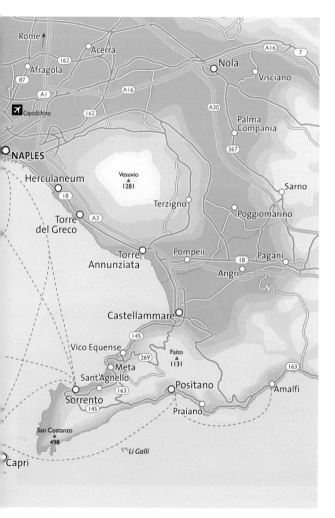

Getting to know the Neapolitan Riviera

The Neapolitan Riviera has been the destination of choice for holidaymakers since the days of the Roman Empire, when the elite of the ancient world converged on the shores of the Bay of Naples for rest and relaxation.

The draw of the region continues today with everyone from blue-collar locals to Hollywood A-listers flocking to the resorts that line the coast in order to bask in the almost-constant sun. Depending on your budget and tastes, there is an ideal place here for everyone. Whether you're a fan of culture-packed itineraries or if you just like to top up your tan in elegant surroundings, the Neapolitan Riviera will appeal.

● *The picturesque Isle of Ischia*

As the focal point for the region, Naples has been a stop on many 'must-see' lists ever since the time when a European grand tour was an essential for every sophisticated society member. The city continues to attract visitors due to its wealth of artefacts, great dining options, elegant shopping and 'real people' buzz. A stroll through the streets of Spaccanapoli or the Centro Storico (Old Town) puts you in touch with southern Italy's authentic vibe, complete with washing hanging on the lines across city streets, gossiping neighbours in the doorways, children kicking a ball around, and pious black-clad grandmothers on their way to pray at one of the hundreds of glorious churches dotted throughout the metropolis.

If you want to explore the ancient ruins of Pompeii and Herculaneum, not to mention the imposing volcanic Vesuvius, then Naples is your perfect base. And if you still haven't had your fill of Roman history, there are plenty of archaeological treats right beneath your feet in Naples itself.

If you're looking for chic elegance, however, then it is to the islands of Capri, Procida and Ischia that you must venture. Capri has been enchanting visitors for millennia – so much so that it was declared the capital of the Roman Empire for a short period after Tiberius transplanted his court there in AD 26. Ischia, meanwhile, is famed for the healing power of its waters and there are a number of natural spas where you can try them out for yourself. Procida, the baby of the family, attracts bohemians and fans of unspoilt natural beauty.

Sorrento is a popular choice for British tourists looking for a package holiday, with many major tour operators offering this picturesque seaside community as a short break or week-long getaway locale. You can choose to remain in the resort for the duration of your stay – or use it as a base from where you can explore the towns of the Amalfi Coast.

Culture and calm, history and holiday sun – it's all here ready and waiting for you.

THE BEST OF THE NEAPOLITAN RIVIERA

TOP 10 ATTRACTIONS

- **Sipping *limoncello*** *Limoncello* is one of Italy's finest contributions to the global liquor cabinet and Capri is where the first batches were ever made (see page 89).

- **Volcanic encounters** The Campanian coast dances with fate every day due to its position at the base of still-active Mount Vesuvius. A climb up Vesuvius is truly a memorable experience and possible even for novice walkers (see page 75).

- **Pondering Pompeii** Frozen in time due to the eruption that occurred in AD 79, the UNESCO World Heritage Site of Pompeii is a wonder to behold (see page 78).

- **Celebrity-spotting in Capri** Mariah Carey, Keanu Reeves, Demi Moore, Tom Cruise, Julia Roberts, Greta Garbo, Sophia Loren and Clark Gable have soaked up the sun on the tiny island of Capri. See what's so special by following them to the glorious island (see page 35).

- **Football frenzies** Join the throngs in the football stands of SSC Napoli – once home to Diego Maradona (see page 102).

- **A slice of heaven** Neapolitans claim to have invented pizza. You won't deny this fact once you've seen the wealth of options on regional menus. Simply delicious (see page 91).

- **Bayside promenades** A stroll along the seaside is a must for courting couples, sociable families and grannies on their constitutionals. There's nothing quite like a walk along the Riviera di Chiaia in Naples to make you fall in love with Italy (see page 102).

- **Shopping sensations** Designer goods in Naples and Capri, beautiful woodwork in Sorrento, handmade stationery in Amalfi, organic cheeses and delectable wines – it's all here for you to enjoy (see page 95).

- **A night at the opera** Many connoisseurs report that Naples's Teatro di San Carlo is second only to Milan's La Scala in terms of musical quality and sheer splendour. Find out why by securing a ticket (see page 18).

- **Float your boat** Depending on your budget, you can charter a yacht in Procida's harbour or simply dart around from port to port on one of the regular ferries. Either will put the wind in your hair and allow you to breathe in the sea air (see page 24).

🔻 *Ruins of Pompeii backing on to Mount Vesuvius*

SYMBOLS KEY

The following symbols are used throughout this book:

ⓐ address **ⓣ** telephone **ⓦ** website address
ⓛ opening times **ⓘ** important

The following symbols are used on the maps:

Ⓜ metro		○ city
𝒊 information office		○ large town
✉ post office		○ small town
🛍 shopping		■ POI (point of interest)
✈ airport		= motorway
➕ hospital		— main road
🛡 police station		= minor road
🚌 bus station		— railway
🚆 railway station		
✝ church		

❶ numbers denote featured cafés, restaurants & evening venues

RESTAURANT CATEGORIES

Restaurants in this guide are graded by approximate price as follows:

£ = up to €15   **££** = €15–€25   **£££** = over €25

This refers to the cost of a meal per person excluding wine, taxes and service.

▶ *Amalfi is a typical Neapolitan town*

 RESORTS

Places under the sun

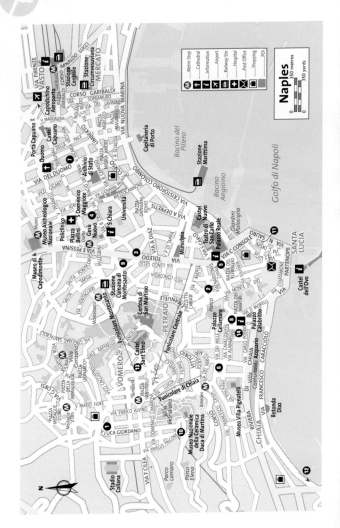

Naples

As the capital of Campania and the metropolis of the Neapolitan Riviera, the city of Naples sometimes gets a bad rap. True, it was notorious for petty theft and violence during the 1980s, but much has been done to spruce up the city in order to make it a more palatable destination for the modern-day traveller.

To enjoy your stay in Naples, you must banish your own sensibilities, and resign yourself to the fact that locals do things in their own time – whether that be driving through the streets (insanely fast) or offering service in an upmarket boutique (painfully slow). Considering the number of times the city has come close to destruction, this *laissez-faire* characteristic is understandable – residents need it in order to survive!

Once the largest metropolis in Europe, Naples has served as the capital for a number of empires during its long and proud history. Numerous castles, museums and palaces attest to its former importance, giving the city a wide range of cultural and artistic locations.

Visitors to the Riviera often get out of Naples as fast as they possibly can to rush to the more salubrious resorts in the Bay of Naples or along the Amalfi Coast. To do this is to miss the pulsating heart of southern Italy – complete with all the chaos and creativity that entails. For bohemians, there is nothing like a day wandering the streets of the Centro Storico (Old Town), admiring the treasures at the Museo Archeologico (Archaeological Museum) and pulling up a chair at one of the cafés that line the Piazza Bellini. Shoppers, meanwhile, will challenge their wallets with a stroll up the Via Toledo or through the designer-studded lanes of Chiaia. Bigger is better after all!

THINGS TO SEE & DO

Castel dell'Ovo (Castle of the Egg)

Naples's oldest castle was built during the Norman period, yet never fulfilled its intended use as a military stronghold until recently. Today it is an administrative centre for the Italian armed forces, although many

rooms, including the viewing platforms, are open to the public.
ⓐ Via Partenope ❶ 081 240 0055 ● 08.00–19.30 Mon–Sat,
08.00–14.00 Sun

Castel Nuovo (New Castle)

It may be called the Castel Nuovo (New Castle), but its history dates back
to the 15th century when it was commissioned by Charles of Anjou.
ⓐ Piazza Municipio ❶ 081 795 5877 Ⓦ www.comune.napoli.it
● 09.00–19.00 Mon–Sat June–Mar; 09.00–18.00 Mon–Sat, 09.00–13.00
Sun Apr & May; ticket office closes 1 hour earlier ❶ Admission charge

Castel Sant'Elmo (Sant'Elmo Castle)

Enjoy stunning views of the Bay of Naples at this castle located on the
edges of the hilltop community of Vomero.
ⓐ Via Tito Angelini 22 ❶ 081 578 4030 ● 09.00–19.30 Wed–Mon; ticket
office closes 1 hour earlier ❶ Admission charge

Duomo (Cathedral)

Naples's most important church is awe-inspiring all year round, but it
truly comes into its own on 19 September when the city celebrates its
patron saint, San Gennaro.
ⓐ Via del Duomo 147 ❶ 081 449 097 Ⓦ www.duomodinapoli.com
● Church: 08.00–12.30, 16.30–19.00 Mon–Sat, 08.00–13.30, 17.00–19.30
Sun; Archaeological area & baptistery: 09.00–12.00, 16.30–18.30
Mon–Sat, 08.30–13.00 Sun ❶ Church: free admission for museum,
archaeological area and baptistery only

Museo di Capodimonte (Capodimonte Museum)

Stunning art can be spotted at this unmissable gallery that boasts
masterpieces by Raphael, Titian, Botticelli, El Greco, Renoir, Caravaggio,
Rembrandt, Tintoretto and the Breughels.
ⓐ Porta Grande, Via Capodimonte ❶ 081 749 9111
Ⓦ www.napolibeniculturali.it ● 10.00–19.00 Tues–Sat, 09.00–14.00 Sun
❶ Admission charge

🔺 *The Museo di Capodimonte, which houses many masterpieces*

Museo Archeologico Nazionale (National Museum of Archaeology)

Europe's finest collection of Roman antiquities is found at this former school, owned and used by Naples University. The bulk of the treasures taken from Herculaneum and Pompeii can be found on the first floor centred on the Sala Meridiana.

ⓐ Piazza Museo 19 ❶ 081 442 2149 Ⓦ www.marketplace.it/museo.nazionale 🕓 09.00–19.30 Wed–Mon, ticket office closes 1 hour earlier ❶ Admission charge

Palazzo Reale (Royal Palace)

More noted for its architecture than its art collections, this palace held both the Spanish viceroys and Bourbon kings. Built in 1600, extensions have since given it a neoclassical façade.

ⓐ Piazza del Plebiscito 1 ❶ 081 580 8111 Ⓦ www.palazzorealenapoli.it 🕓 09.00–20.00 Thur–Tues, ticket office closes 1 hour earlier ❶ Admission charge

Teatro di San Carlo (San Carlo Theatre)

The second-best opera house in Italy. Only Milan's La Scala can compete – and many say it's a close call. Premieres bring out the who's who of Neapolitan society.

ⓐ Via San Carlo 98F ❶ 081 797 2331 Ⓦ www.teatrosancarlo.it 🕓 Box office open Mon–Sat 10.00–19.00 and 1 hour before performances ❶ Admission charge

TAKING A BREAK

Bars & cafés

Bellavia £ ❶ Traditional cakes and biscuits made by Naples's best *pasticceria* (patisserie). ⓐ Via Luca Giordano 158 ❶ 081 578 9684 🕓 08.00–21.30 Tues–Sun ❶ Closed Aug

Brandi £ ❷ Brandi claims to have invented the pizza Margherita in honour of Italy's Queen Margherita in 1889. Famous diners have included

Bill Clinton. **ⓐ** Salita Sant'Anna di Palazzo 1 **ⓣ** 081 416 928
ⓦ www.brandi.it **ⓛ** 12.30–15.00, 19.30–24.00 **ⓘ** Closed 1 week in Aug

Gelateria della Scimmia £ ❸ Naples's oldest and most established
gelateria (ice cream shop). **ⓐ** Piazza Carità 4 **ⓣ** 081 552 0272
ⓛ 10.00–24.00

Gran Caffè Aragonese £ ❹ This bohemian café is often packed with
artists, students and philosophers. **ⓐ** Piazza San Domenico Maggiore 5/8
ⓣ 081 552 8740 **ⓦ** www.grancaffearagonese.it **ⓛ** 07.30–24.00

Caffè Gambrinus £–££ ❺ A fantastic location and years of history make
this café a favourite with tourists and locals alike. Oscar Wilde is
reputed to have been a fan. **ⓐ** Via Chiaia 1–2 **ⓣ** 081 417 582
ⓦ www.caffegambrinus.com **ⓛ** 07.00–01.00

Restaurants
Osteria da Tonino £–££ ❻ Simple, flavourful meals for those on a
budget. **ⓐ** Via Santa Teresa a Chiaia 47 **ⓣ** 081 421 533 **ⓛ** 12.30–16.00
Mon–Sat June, July & Sept; 12.30–16.00 Sun–Wed, 12.30–16.00,
20.00–23.00 Thur–Sat Oct–May **ⓘ** Closed 2 weeks in Aug

Antica Osteria Pisano ££ ❼ Intimate restaurant featuring the best in
Neapolitan specialities. Tours of the kitchen are available.
ⓐ Piazzetta Crocelle ai Mannesi 1 **ⓣ** 081 554 8325 **ⓛ** 12.00–16.00,
19.00–23.00 Mon–Sat **ⓘ** Closed Aug

Umberto ££ ❽ The best vegetarian restaurant in town. Gluten-free
options are also available. **ⓐ** Via Alabardieri 30/31 **ⓣ** 081 418 555
ⓦ www.umberto.it **ⓛ** 12.00–16.00, 19.00–23.30 Tues–Sun
ⓘ Closed 3 weeks in Aug

La Vecchia Cantina ££ ❾ Fish so fresh, it's still wriggling on the plate
thanks to this restaurant's location immediately next to the fish market.

@ Via San Nicola alla Carità 13–14 ❶ 081 552 0226 ❷ 12.00–15.00, 20.00–23.00 Mon & Wed–Sat, 12.00–15.30 Tues & Sun

D'Angelo Santa Caterina ££–£££ ❿ Romantic dining spot set within lush gardens and boasting glorious city views. @ Via Aniello Falcone 203 ❶ 081 578 9772 Ⓦ www.ristorantedangelo.com ❷ 19.30–22.30 Mon & Wed–Sat, 13.00–15.30 Sun ❶ Closed 2 weeks in Aug

AFTER DARK

Restaurants
La Cantinella £££ ⓫ The restaurant of choice for special occasions – especially if you love seafood. @ Via Nazario Sauro 23 ❶ 081 764 8684 Ⓦ www.lacantinella.it ❷ 12.30–15.00, 19.30–23.30 Mon–Sat ❶ Closed 2 weeks in Aug

Donnanna £££ ⓬ Elegant dining thanks to the organic menu and refined ambience. @ Via Posillipo 16B ❶ 081 769 0920 ❷ 12.30–15.00 Sun, 12.00–15.00, 19.00–23.00 Tues–Sat

Bars
Miami Bar Room ⓭ Minimalist bar serving great cocktails in sleek surroundings. @ Via Morghen 68c ❶ 081 229 8332 ❷ 22.00–04.00 Wed–Sun ❶ Closed July–Sept

Clubs
S'move ⓮ Always packed with Neapolitan party people, this is the place to see and be seen. @ Vico dei Sospiri 10A ❶ 081 764 5813 Ⓦ www.smove-lab.net ❷ 19.30–02.00 daily ❶ Closed Aug

One of Naples' typical narrow streets

Procida

Of the three famous islands in the Bay of Naples, Procida is the least well known and least visited. That's not to say it doesn't get crowds – it certainly does during the peak summer months – but its charm comes from its intimacy and personal feel compared to its more well-heeled neighbours. Bohemians and artists adore Procida due to the island's small size and lack of pretensions. Boating enthusiasts also flock here as there are a number of operators offering yacht rentals either for just a day or for a more extended period.

Procida's reputation as a hidden secret may not last much longer, however, as a number of condo developments are beginning to transform the topography and personality of the area. If you have the chance, see it now before it becomes yet another built-up beachside community.

BEACHES

Lido di Procida
Every Italian resort has a beach that is more about who is seeing you than how to relax. In Procida, this is the place to show off your tan lines (or lack thereof).
ⓐ Just off Marina di Chiaiolella

Pozzo Vecchio
If you've seen the film *Il Postino*, then this beach may look familiar. The walk to reach it through lemon groves is especially pleasant.
ⓐ Below Via Flavio Gioia

Spiaggia di Chiaia
Procida has very few beaches to enjoy, and this is probably the best if you're after a plot of sand.
ⓐ South off Via Pizzaco

⬥ *Procida harbour*

THINGS TO SEE & DO

Abbazia di San Michele Arcangelo (San Michele Arcangelo Abbey)

This 11th-century church, built almost directly into the rock face, has been remodelled throughout the centuries and boasts a collection of religious manuscripts, a historic nativity scene and a catacomb maze that once served as the local cemetery. The famous Good Friday procession held annually on the island starts at the church's entrance.

ⓐ Via Terra Murata 89 ❶ 081 896 7612 ⓦ www.abbaziasanmichele.it
🕒 10.00–12.45, 15.00–18.00 Mon–Sat, 09.45–12.45 Sun

Castello d'Avalos (Avalos Castle)

It may look like a desolate ruin today, but this formidable structure was known as Italy's version of Alcatraz until 1986. Even so, many prisoners requested a transfer here in order to enjoy the inspiring views.

ⓐ Via Terra Murata ❶ The building is not open to the public. Despite this, the panoramas from the grounds continue to draw visitors

Marina Grande (Main Harbour)

Compared to Ischia and Capri, Procida is a decidedly sleepy destination. Due to its peacefulness, it is a major draw for artists and bohemians looking for

> **FLOAT YOUR BOAT**
> Of all the resorts in Campania, this is probably the best from which you can charter your own yacht or enjoy a boat trip. Two operators of note are:
> **Blue Dream** Charter your own yacht and feel like a true mariner at this establishment offering various craft starting from just €60 per day.
> ⓐ Via Vittorio Emanuele 14 ❶ 081 896 0579 ⓦ bluedreamcharter.com
> **Ippocampo** Wooden boat hires offered at around €75 per day.
> ⓐ Marina Chiaiolella ❶ 081 658 7667 ⓦ www.ippocampo.biz

⬥ *Enjoy a yacht trip around Procida's Marina Grande*

inspiration without all the pretentiousness of other locales. When you're in need of a bit of human interaction and late-night fun, head to the Marina Grande to watch the throngs go by. August is especially busy.

Santa Maria della Pietà
An intimate 18th-century church worth entering if in search of some solitude.
ⓐ Via Roma 164 ❶ 081 896 7005 ● 08.30–12.00, 16.00–20.00

TAKING A BREAK

Bars & cafés
Bar Roma £ Coffee and cake that seems to get divine inspiration from the church of Santa Maria della Pietà next door. ⓐ Via Roma 163 ❶ 081 896 7460 ● 07.00–24.00 Wed–Mon

Restaurants
Il Cantinone £–££ There is a full menu at this restaurant on Marina Grande, but most come for the pizza – and for good reason.
ⓐ Via Roma 55–58 ❶ 081 896 8811 ● 12.00–15.00, 19.30–23.00 Wed–Mon
❶ Closed mid-Jan–Feb

Fammivento £–££ Soak in the sun at this buzzing eatery located right on the Marina Grande. For somewhere as central as this, you would expect small portions; luckily, this restaurant bucks the trend. ⓐ Via Roma 39
❶ 081 896 9020 ● 12.30–15.30, 19.00–23.00 Tues–Sun Mar–Dec
❶ Closed Jan & Feb

La Pergola ££ Petite restaurant situated in a tranquil garden using only locally produced ingredients. ⓐ Via V Rinaldi 37 ❶ 081 896 9534
● 19.00–23.00 Tues–Sun mid-Apr–Oct ❶ Closed Nov–mid-Apr

AFTER DARK

Restaurants

Conchiglia ££ Formal dining room serving specialities of the island in an old-fashioned environment. Think crisp linens and besuited waiters for an idea of what to expect. ⓐ Via Pizzaco, Discesa Graziella ⓣ 081 896 7602 ⓦ www.laconchigliaristorante.com ⓛ 12.30–15.00, 19.30–23.00 Apr–Oct ⓘ Closed Nov–Mar

Crescenzo ££ This romantic dining spot overlooks the picturesque bay of Chiaiolella and seduces with both the atmosphere and the food. ⓐ Via Marina di Chiaiolelle 33 ⓣ 081 896 7255 ⓦ www.hotelcrescenzo.it ⓛ 12.30–14.30, 19.30–22.30 Apr–Oct ⓘ Closed Tues Nov–Mar

Bars

Bar del Cavaliere £–££ When searching for a tipple, go straight to this popular bar – considered the best on the island. ⓐ Via Roma 42 ⓣ 081 810 1074 ⓛ 07.00–03.00 Apr–Sept; 12.30–15.30, 19.00–23.00 Tues–Sun Oct–Mar

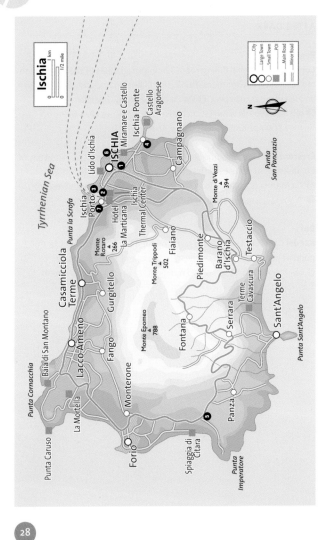

Ischia

Tyrrhenian Sea

Punta Cornacchia

Punta Caruso

La Mortella

Baia di San Montano

Lacco Ameno

Forio

Spiaggia di Citara

Punta Imperatore

Casamicciola Terme

Gurgitello

Fango

Monterone

Monte Epomeo 788

Punta la Scrofa

Ischia Porto

Lido d'Ischia

ISCHIA

Miramare e Castello

Ischia Ponte

Castello Aragonese

Campagnano

Punta San Pancrazio

Monte di Vezzi 394

Hotel La Marticana

Ischia Thermal Center

Monte Rotaro 266

Monte Trippodi 502

Fiaiano

Piedimonte

Barano d'Ischia

Testaccio

Fontana

Serrara

Terme Cavascura

Sant'Angelo

Panza

Punta Sant'Angelo

① ② ③ ④ ⑤ ⑥ ⑦

City
Large Town
Small Town
POI
Main Road
Minor Road

N

1 km
1/2 mile
0
0

28

Ischia

Holidaymakers have been coming to Ischia since its thermal waters were discovered to have beneficial health effects in the 8th century BC. Visitors flock here, eager to enjoy the laid-back pace and relaxing spas. So desired was this rocky outcrop that the Angevins, Aragonese and British all fought over it at some point during its often violent history – in fact, you can still see the bullet holes in the walls of the Castello Aragonese from the British bombardment of the 19th century.

Ischia and Capri often battle it out in terms of celebrity pulling power, with Capri attracting young starlets and Ischia aimed more at the established *grandes dames* of the entertainment industry. To fully appreciate the island, get away from the main port and explore the interior and far coastlines where the beaches are unspoilt and the vegetation is lush and green.

▲ *La Mortella gardens in Ischia*

BEACHES

Baia di San Montano (San Montano Bay)

A good locale for family trips due to the shallow, clear waters, just a hop away from the healing waters and peaceful gardens of Negombo.
ⓐ West of Lacco Ameno

Lido d'Ischia

If your ideal beach involves people-watching and non-stop action, then set up your towel at this beach close to Ischia's main ferry port. While the water and sand aren't as good as others you might find on the island, you're only a short stroll away from the main town's action.
ⓐ East of Ischia Town port

Punta Caruso (Caruso Point)

Only strong swimmers should attempt to come to this secluded bathing spot known for its privacy and deep waters.
ⓐ Follow the path running from Via Guardiola

Spiaggia di Citara

Forio has a long beach – but many feel it is too crowded. Instead, head south to this stretch of sand. For a premium spot, consider paying for a space at the Giardini Poseidon.
ⓐ South of Forio Town

THINGS TO SEE & DO

Castello Aragonese (Aragon Castle)

Fortified with a castle since the 5th century, this outcrop has been used as a stronghold by many occupying forces, including the Goths, Romans and British. Inside there is a distinctly gruesome museum showcasing historical instruments of torture.
ⓐ Piazzale Aragonese ❶ 081 992 834 ⓦ www.castelloaragonese.it
🕓 09.00–19.30 ❶ Admission charge

⬧ The dramatic Castello Aragonese

La Mortella

Over 3,000 plant species – many of them rare – are housed in these beautiful gardens.
ⓐ Via F Calise 39, Forio ⓣ 081 986 220 ⓦ www.lamortella.org
ⓛ 09.00–19.00 Tues, Thur, Sat & Sun Apr–June, Sept–mid-Nov;
09.00–20.00 July & Aug ⓘ Closed mid-Nov–Apr

TAKING A BREAK

Bars & cafés

Bar Calise £ ❶ Scrumptious ice cream and cakes – don't miss it!
ⓐ Piazza degli Eroi 69 ⓣ 081 991 270 ⓛ 07.00–02.00 Apr–Oct;
07.00–02.00 Thur–Tues Nov–Mar

Da Ciccio £ ❷ Delicious ice cream that draws fans from miles around.
ⓐ Via Porto 1 ⓣ 081 991 314 ⓛ 07.00–02.00 Mar–Oct; 07.00–24.00
Tues–Sun Nov–Feb

Pane & Vino £ ❸ Stock up at this bread and wine shop for ferry
crossing days or when you just want a picnic.
ⓐ Via Porto 24 ⓣ 081 991 046 ⓛ 10.00–02.00 Apr–Oct; 10.00–13.00,
16.30–21.30 Thur–Tues Nov–mid-Jan & Mar ⓘ Closed mid-Jan–Feb

Cocò ££ ❹ Seafood and pasta – often served to locals who call this
place a favourite. ⓐ Piazzale Aragonese 1 ⓣ 081 981 823 ⓛ 12.30–15.00,
19.30–23.00 May–Sept; 12.30–15.00, 19.30–23.00 Thur–Tues Mar, Apr &
Oct–Dec ⓘ Closed Jan & Feb

AFTER DARK

Restaurants

Cantine di Pietratorcia £££ ❺ The best wine cellar on the island can be
found at this winery set among the greenery of the island. Book in
advance to enjoy the full menu. ⓐ Via Provinciale Panza 267

🆃 081 907 232 🅦 www.pietratorcia.it 🅛 17.30–late mid-June–mid-Sept; 10.00–13.00, 16.00–20.00 Mon–Thur, 10.00–13.00, 16.00–late Fri–Sun Apr–mid-June & mid-Sept–mid-Nov ❶ Closed mid-Nov–Mar

Restaurante Alberto Ischia £££ ❻ Inspiring food served on a platform that overlooks the sea – especially good at sunset. 🅐 Via Cristoforo Colombo 8 🆃 081 981 259 🅦 www.albertoischia.it 🅛 12.00–15.00, 19.30–23.00 ❶ Closed Nov–mid-Mar

Bars
Osteria del Porto £–££ ❼ Situated on the port of Ischia, overlooking the fishing boats. 🅐 Riva destra–Via Porto 91–93 🆃 081 901 841 🅦 www.osteriadelporto.it 🅛 18.00–02.00 mid-Mar–Jan

---

THE SPAS OF ISCHIA
There are over 150 spas on Ischia drawing health-replenishing waters from the 56 mineral springs that are dotted throughout the island's topography. If you are looking to include a soak in your stay, check hotel packages in advance to see if spa options are included. A couple of the better spas include:

Ischia Thermal Center
State-of-the-art spa centre on Ischia boasting the latest facilities and treatments. 🅐 Via Delle Terme 15 🆃 081 984 376 🅦 www.ischiathermalcenter.it 🅛 08.30–17.30

Terme Cavascura
Dating back to Roman times, this spa is one of the originals. Many of the pools are carved out from the grottos and caves on which the site is located. 🅐 Via Cavascura 1 🆃 081 905 564 🅦 www.cavascura.it 🅛 08.30–13.30, 14.30–18.00 mid-Apr–Oct ❶ Closed Nov–mid-Apr

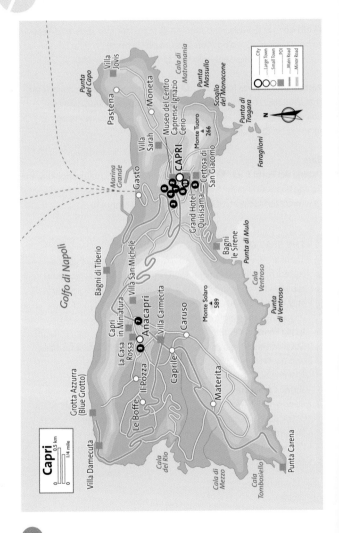

Capri

Bold and brash or elegant and sophisticated? You can decide after a visit to this glamorous island that was once proclaimed capital of the Roman Empire. In AD 27, Emperor Tiberius arrived on Capri and fell so in love with the place that he built 12 villas, each dedicated to the major gods of the Roman religion, and moved his court to the island. Rumours about the levels of depravity in his adopted homes soon spread across the Empire until his untimely death ten years later.

Never one to shy away from scandal, Capri has welcomed a number of characters and bohemians to its shores over the centuries, the most notable being the writer W.H. Auden, who was driven off Capri following reports of his trysts with a teenage boy. His departure marked the end of a gay era that flourished during the first three decades of the 20th century.

Today, Capri is divided in half by two communities: Capri with its designer boutiques, top-end hotels and see-and-be-seen mentality; and Anacapri, the more laid-back and unspoiled village with a decidedly 'real people' feel.

🔺 *Capri harbour*

Also of note is Capri's most famous sight, the **Grotta Azzurra** (Blue Grotto). The mysterious blue from which the grotto gets its name is caused by light refraction on the cave walls. Regular boat services take day-trippers inside the cave from the Marina Grande.

Whether you are staying for an extended period or just for a couple of hours, a visit to one of the four cafés on the piazzetta in Capri Town is an absolute must. While the prices are sinfully inflated, it's the best people-watching spot in the Neapolitan Riviera. Be sure to order a glass of the local liqueur *limoncello*, which was originally produced here in Capri.

BEACHES

For an island this famous, you would expect it to be packed with glorious beaches. Unfortunately, this is not the case, with most swimming spots either reserved by private hotels or covered in sharp pebbles. Despite this, there are a few public swimming locales to dip your toes in. The best are:

Bagni di Tiberio (Tiberius's Baths)
Go to the north side of Capri island to reach this sandy beach that is open to all.
🅰 Take a boat from Marina Grande

Bagni le Sirene (Sirens' Baths)
Close to Marina Piccola is this beach club for which you will have to pay a moderate entrance fee.
🅰 Marina Piccola 🕿 081 837 0221 🕒 Hours vary ❶ Admission charge

Punta Carena (Carena Point)
Popular with the locals, this beach is actually a cluster of rocks situated near the lighthouse. In summer, you should avoid going at weekends when it gets extremely busy.
🅰 Base of the lighthouse

THINGS TO SEE & DO

Capri in Miniatura (Capri in Miniature)

Distract the tots for a few minutes with this miniature scale model of the island carved out of rock.

🄰 Via G Orlandi 105, Anacapri 🄣 081 837 1169 🄛 09.00–18.00
🄘 Admission charge. At time of going to press, the structure was undergoing restoration work. Due to reopen 2010.

Certosa di San Giacomo (Charterhouse of St James)

This collection of buildings was originally built in the 14th century and consisted of a church, cloister and garden. While the architecture is intriguing, most are drawn by the glorious views.

🄰 Via Certosa, Capri 🄣 081 837 6218 🄛 09.00–14.00 Tues–Sun

Grotta Azzurra (Blue Grotto)

Capri's most famous sight is also home to a great swimming hole. Dive in from the platform located near the main entrance of the cave. Poets have raved about the mysterious blue colour created by the refraction of the light on the walls of this inspiring grotto.

🄰 Tours can be arranged from the Marina Grande 🄛 09.00–1 hour before sunset

La Casa Rossa (The Red House)

Eclectic collection of paintings and artefacts pieced together by the 19th-century American colonel who built the red house in which the exhibits are held.

🄰 Via G Orlandi, Anacapri 🄣 081 837 2193 🄛 10.30–13.30, 17.30–21.00
🄘 Admission charge

Monte Solaro (Mount Solaro)

Take the 12-minute chairlift ride to the top of this mountain and enjoy amazing views over the Bay of Naples. On clear days, you can even see Mount Vesuvius looming in the distance.

◆ *Boats entering Grotta Azzurra*

🅐 Via Caposcuro 10 ☎ 081 837 1428 🕒 09.30–17.00 Mar–Oct; 10.00–15.30 Nov–Feb ❶ Admission charge

Museo e Biblioteca del Centro Caprense Ignazio Cerio (Museum and Library of the Ignazio Cerio Centre of Capri)

This museum features artefacts that tell the story of Capri's earliest years before the arrival of the Greeks and Romans. Good for a rainy day.

🅐 Piazzetta Cerio 5 ☎ 081 837 6681 🌐 www.culturacampania.rai.it
🕒 Museum: 10.00–13.00 Tues–Sat. Library: 09.30–13.00 Wed & Sat; 17.30–20.00 Tues, Thur, Fri ❶ Admission charge for museum

Villa Damecuta

Less impressive than the Villa Jovis, this villa is another of Tiberius's famed residences – although time has not been so kind. Little remains except for the wonderful views over Ischia.

🅐 Grotta Azzurra bus from Anacapri ☎ No phone
🌐 www.capri.com/en/damecuta 🕒 09.00–1 hour before sunset

Villa Jovis

Tiberius built 12 villas on the island – each one dedicated to the most important gods of the Roman Empire. This is the best preserved of the lot. Who knows what depraved goings-on happened in these rooms over 2,000 years ago!

🅐 2.4 km (1½ miles) northeast of Capri Town, Viale Amedeo Maiuri
☎ No phone 🌐 www.capri.com/en/villa-jovis 🕒 09.00–sunset
❶ Admission charge

Villa San Michele

Built in the 19th century, this villa was once home to a Swedish doctor and writer. The gardens and views are the reason to visit.

🅐 Viale Axel Munthe 34 ☎ 081 837 1401 🌐 www.sanmichele.org
🕒 09.00–18.00 May–Sept; 09.00–17.00 Oct & Apr; 09.00–15.30 Nov–Feb; 09.00–16.30 Mar ❶ Admission charge

TAKING A BREAK

Bars & cafés
Al Piccolo Bar ££ ❶ The Piazzetta has always been the place of choice to see and be seen – but this bar (one of four on the square) is the local favourite. For public displays, sit at one of the tables on the square; otherwise go upstairs and watch the beautiful people as they pass below you unawares. ⓐ Piazzetta Umberto 1 ❶ 081 837 0325 ⏱ 06.00–02.00 Apr–Oct; 06.00–22.00 Nov–Mar

Restaurants
La Cisterna £ ❷ Finding cheap, tasty food on Capri can be a challenge. This pizzeria embraces the challenge, turning out great local favourites and delicious Margheritas. ⓐ Via Madre Serafina 5 ❶ 081 837 5620 ⏱ 12.00–15.30, 19.00–24.00 (summer); 11.30–14.00, 18.30–23.00 (winter)

La Pergola £ ❸ Cheap and cheerful alfresco eatery offering classic takes on traditional dishes. ⓐ Via Traversa Lo Palazzo 2 ❶ 081 837 7414 ⏱ 12.30–15.00, 19.30–23.00 daily Apr–Oct; 12.30–15.00, 19.30–23.00 Thur–Tues Nov–Mar ❶ Closed mid-Nov–25 Dec

Al Grottino ££ ❹ Back in the 1950s, this was *the* place to get a meal. It may have lost its A-list status, but it still churns out solid takes on Caprese favourites. ⓐ Via Longano 27 ❶ 081 837 0584 ⏱ 12.00–15.00, 18.30–24.00 ❶ Closed Nov–Mar

Il Geranio £££ ❺ Located in a beautifully restored 18th-century mansion, this restaurant offers a daily-changing menu in warm surroundings. ⓐ Viale Matteoti 8 ❶ 081 837 0616 ⓦ www.geraniocapri.com ⏱ 12.30–15.00, 19.30–00.30 daily Apr–Nov

AFTER DARK

Restaurants

La Capannina £££ ❻ Intimate and romantic – this restaurant has been a favourite among Capri's élite ever since it opened in the 1930s. ⓐ Via Le Botteghe 12 bis-14 ❶ 081 837 0732 Ⓦ www.capannina.capri.com ❶ 12.00–15.00, 19.30–24.00 May–Sept; 12.00–14.00, 19.30–24.00 Thur–Tues mid-Mar ❶ Closed 2nd week in Nov–mid-Mar

Olivo of the Capri Palace £££ ❼ Many islanders feel that this restaurant is the best on the island. Unlike other high-priced eateries, chef Oliver Glowig takes risks in his cooking and menu selections – and the rewards are high indeed. Menus change daily and always use only the finest of fresh, regional, organic ingredients. ⓐ Via Capodimonte 2b, Anacapri ❶ 081 978 0111 Ⓦ www.capripalace.com ❶ 12.30–14.30, 19.30–22.30 ❶ Closed Nov–Mar

Villa Verde £££ ❽ Looking to spot a celebrity? Then make your reservation here and dive into traditional yet well-prepared versions of local dishes. ⓐ Vico Sella Orta 6A ❶ 081 837 7024 Ⓦ www.villaverde-capri.com ❶ 12.00–15.30, 19.00–24.00 Apr–Oct ❶ Closed Nov–mid-Dec, early Jan–mid-Mar

Bars

Caffè Michelangelo £ ❾ Relaxing and unpretentious – this is the best place to enjoy a sip of something cold in Anacapri. ⓐ Via G Orlandi 138, Anacapri ❶ 333 778 4331 ❶ 09.00–01.00 ❶ Closed Jan

Taverna Anema e Core £–££ ❿ It may seem like a rustic drinking den, but this is where the A-listers like to come out and play. Expect to fork out many euros if you want to tag along. ⓐ Via Sella Orta 39e ❶ 081 837 6461 Ⓦ www.anemaecore.com ❶ 22.00–04.00 Apr–Oct ❶ Closed Nov–Mar

● *The panoramic view of Sorrento's Marina Piccola*

Sorrento

Purists sometimes argue that Sorrento isn't the 'real' Amalfi Coast. For the average tourist, however, it is often the affordable and accessible gateway to the region. Since the days of the Greek Empire it has been beloved by visitors, but it has always maintained a sort of second-class status on the Neapolitan Riviera because it has never been a major mercantile power or regional capital. Despite this lack of historical importance, its treasures remained largely untouched through the ages as pirates and empires chose to sack more lucrative harbours.

Popular with package tourists, Sorrento has an undeserved reputation as a favourite with British regular holidaymakers who see the town as a 'safe' Italian getaway without the pretensions of Capri or inaccessibility of the Amalfi Coast. Surprisingly, there are few beaches in the town proper. Instead, visitors make do with a network of floating pontoons on which it is possible to rent a deckchair and soak up the sun.

BEACHES

Bagni Regina Giovanna (Queen Giovanna's Baths)
Situated in the middle of a collection of Roman ruins, this peaceful, rocky beach is popular due to its clear waters and inspiring views.
📍 2 km (1¼ miles) west of Sorrento

Marina Grande (Main Harbour)
This seafront area is lined with eateries and houses along its dark sand stretch. For a little more space, rent a deckchair at one of the jetties, although you will have to pay dearly. A day sunning on the pontoons is considered a must for fans of people-watching.
📍 700 m (765 yds) west of Piazza Tasso ❶ In high season, deckchairs can cost as much as €17 a day

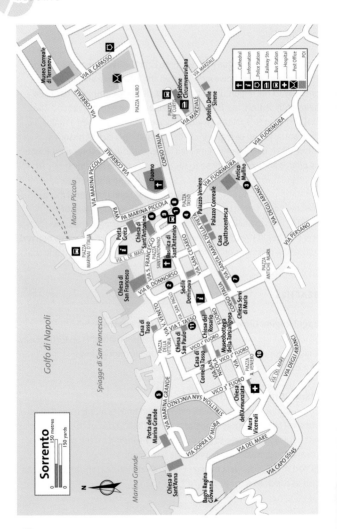

Marina Piccola (Small Harbour)

This tiny piece of beach becomes crowded with posing young Italians.
For a bit of privacy, pay for entrance into one of the private bathing clubs.
ⓐ Centre of Sorrento

Spiagge di San Francesco

Bright pontoons complete with beach huts jut out into the sea from the
base of a cliff below the Villa Communale.
ⓐ Walk down the steep path from the Villa Communale
❶ Admission charge for access to lido

THINGS TO SEE & DO

Basilica di Sant'Antonino (St Anthony's Basilica)

Surprisingly, it is in this much smaller church that you will find the bones of
Sorrento's patron saint – and not in the more celebrated Duomo. There are
whale bones inside the structure to represent one of the miracles St Anthony
is said to have performed in rescuing a child from a whale's stomach.
ⓐ Piazza Sant'Antonino **❶** 081 878 1437 **🕒** 07.00–12.00, 17.00–19.00

Chiesa di San Francesco (Church of St Francis)

Peaceful cloisters that often hold live performances of classical music
during the warm summer months.
ⓐ Via San Francesco **❶** 081 878 1269 **🕒** 06.00–13.00, 16.00–20.00
(open until 22.00 July–Aug)

Duomo (Cathedral)

Sorrento's cathedral is of note for fans of the Gothic style. Of special
interest are the choir stalls featuring *intarsio* (wooden inlay) work.
ⓐ Corso Italia **❶** 081 878 2248 **🕒** 07.45–12.00, 16.30–20.30

Museo Correale di Terranova (Correale di Terranova Museum)

A mish-mash of artefacts offering everything from ancient vases and
marbles through to 18th-century painting. The display of old photos of

◆ *Sorrento's rocky coastline*

Sorrento in the early part of the 20th century are of particular interest.
ⓐ Via Correale 50 ⓣ 081 878 1846 ⓦ www.museocorreale.com
ⓛ 09.00–14.00 Wed–Mon ⓘ Admission charge

Museobottega della Tarsialignea (The Museum of Inlaid Wood)
Exhibits of local handicrafts and masterpieces set in the beautiful
confines of an 18th-century palazzo.
ⓐ Via San Nicola 28 ⓣ 081 877 1942
ⓦ www.alessandrofiorentinocollection.it ⓛ 10.00–13.00, 15.00–18.30
Mon–Sat ⓘ Admission charge

TAKING A BREAK

Bars & cafés
Bar Ercolano £ ❶   Buzzing café that is known for being a great place for
people-watching, rather than for the hastiness of its waiting service.
The tastiness of the nibbles (usually) makes up for the slow service.
ⓐ Piazza Tasso ⓣ 081 807 2951 ⓛ 06.00–01.30 Wed–Mon Apr–Sept;
06.00–22.30 Wed–Mon Oct–Mar

Davide Il Gelato £ ❷   Some say that the ice cream here is the
best in Italy – best try a scoop then, right? ⓐ Via Padre R Giuliani 39
ⓣ 081 878 1337 ⓛ 09.00–02.00 Mar–Oct

Mondo Bio £ ❸   The place might be small, but to vegetarians and
vegans it's a godsend. Also a health-food store, this eatery serves up
organic, tofu and veggie dishes to please the non-carnivore palate and it
offers a takeaway service.
ⓐ Via degli Aranci 146–148 ⓣ 081 807 5694 ⓛ 08.30–20.30 Mon–Sat

Il Fauno £–££ ❹   Definitely the preferred café for the smart set, this
favourite spot offers great people-watching. Prices can be on the high
side. ⓐ Piazza Tasso 13–15 ⓣ 081 878 1135 ⓛ 07.00–24.00 ⓘ Closed
2 weeks in Jan

Restaurants

Da Emilia £ ❺   Unpretentious and simple – this family-run establishment dishes up ample portions of well-made local classics.
ⓐ Via Marina Grande 62 ⓣ 081 807 2720 ⓛ 12.30–15.00, 19.00–23.30 Apr–Nov ⓘ Nov–Mar: Intermittent lunches, check in advance to see if the restaurant is open

Il Buco ££ ❻   Creative menu of beautifully presented Sorrentine delicacies with a twist. Try the tasting menu for a special treat.
ⓐ Rampa Marina Piccola 5 ⓣ 081 878 2354 ⓦ www.ilbucoristorante.it
ⓛ 12.00–15.30, 19.00–23.30

La Stalla ££ ❼   While pasta is on the menu, it's the pizzas that draw the bulk of the crowds. The open-air terrace covered with awnings draped in flowers and blossoms make this the perfect place to rest tired feet on summer afternoons. ⓐ Via Santa Maria della Pietà 30 ⓣ 081 807 4145
ⓛ 12.00–15.00, 19.00–23.30 Thur–Tues

AFTER DARK

Restaurants

Ristorante Vittoria ££ ❽   Very old-fashioned restaurant that feels like it is a little out of place in modern times. Dishes can surprise or disappoint, depending on how the chef is feeling. But it's the fussy service and 'Olde Worlde' charm that keeps people coming back. Choose between eating in the lavish dining room with frescoed ceilings or on the terrace overlooking the coast.
ⓐ Grand Hotel Excelsior Vittoria, Piazza Tasso 34 ⓣ 081 807 1044
ⓦ www.exvitt.it/sorrento_restaurant.html ⓛ 13.00–14.15, 19.45–22.30

Caruso ££–£££ ❾   Seasonal menu of Sorrentine treasures dedicated to the famed tenor of the same name who holidayed frequently on the peninsula. ⓐ Via Sant'Antonino 12 ⓣ 081 807 3156
ⓦ www.ristorantemuseocaruso.com ⓛ 12.00–24.00

Bars

Insolito £ 🔟 Minimalist white interiors make this late-opening bar popular with young hipsters. ⓐ Corso Italia 38E ☎ 081 877 2409 ⓦ www.insolitosorrento.it 🕐 07.30–04.00

The Garden ££ 🔟 Well-stocked wine bar offering great people-watching and platters of fine prosciutto and local cheeses. For larger meals and home-made desserts, head for the upstairs floor. ⓐ Via T Tasso 2 ☎ 081 878 1195 ⓦ www.thegardenrestaurant.it 🕐 12.00–15.00, 18.30–23.30 Tues–Sun ❗ Closed mid-Jan–Feb

🔺 *Sorrento town by day*

Sorrentine Peninsula: the north coast

East of Sorrento lie the towns of the Sorrentine Peninsula's north coast, a collection of towns that blur into a sprawl of holiday resorts.
The first stop along the coast is Sant'Agnello, a town notable only for its main street and a few holiday villas. Further out of town is where the good stuff begins, including a number of attractive beaches and archaeological sites of interest.

Meta di Sorrento is the place to head for if you're looking for a beach where you can dip your toes. Not only is it the largest stretch of sand in the region, it also boasts a Saracen watchtower of historical interest.

The highlight of the coast is Vico Equense, an important community during the Roman period until it was destroyed by raiding Goths in the 5th century. Today, it is an important wine-growing region known for the quality of its reds.

BEACHES

Calcare
The site of a former lime quarry that operated here for centuries until the 19th century, this beach is overlooked by a Saracen watchtower.
ⓐ West from the Marina di Equa, in Meta di Sorrento

Marina di Equa
Three beaches are within spitting distance of this harbour located to the west of Vico Equense. The beach at Pezzolo is of particular interest due to its proximity to the ruins of a 1st-century AD Roman ruin.
ⓐ West of Vico Equense harbour

Marina di Vico
Small pebble-strewn beach lined with forgettable restaurants. Good for a brief dip.
ⓐ Near the Metro del Mare, east of Vico Equense town centre

● *View across the hillside to Vico Equense and Mt Vesuvius beyond*

> **WALKING THE PENINSULA**
> The north coast is the starting point for numerous trails going
> inland towards the Amalfi Coast. For hikes in the Monte Faito
> region and onwards to Positano, head to Moiano to begin your trek.

Spiaggia di Alimuri

The region's longest stretch of sand is this beach located near
Meta di Sorrento. On summer days, the entire strip can become
extremely crowded.

ⓐ East of Sorrento at Meta di Sorrento

THINGS TO SEE & DO

Antiquarium Aequano (Aequano Antiquities Collection)

A number of finds from a nearby necropolis dating from between the
7th and 5th centuries BC are displayed in this collection located in the
town hall.

ⓐ Palazzo Municipale, Corso Filangieri 98, Vico Equense ⓣ 081 801 9111
ⓛ By appointment only

Madonna del Lauro

Rebuilt in the 18th century, this basilica is rumoured to stand over the
site of a temple to Minerva. The façade is neoclassical in design,
overlooking the main square of Meta di Sorrento.

ⓐ Piazza Meta di Sorrento ⓣ No phone ⓛ 07.00–12.00, 16.00–19.00

Museo Archeologico Georges Vallet
(Georges Vallet Archaeological Museum), Villa Fondi

This museum is a pleasant enough diversion on rainy days, packed with
archaeological finds gathered from across the Sorrentine Peninsula. In
summer, a concert schedule brings crowds to its grounds.

ⓐ Via Ripa di Cassano 14, Piano di Sorrento ⓣ 081 808 7078
ⓛ 09.00–19.00 Tues–Sun

Museo Mineralogico Campano (Campanian Minerals Museum)
Geologists will find the collection at this mineral museum of interest, especially the finds from Vesuvius. Science buffs will love it.
ⓐ Via San Ciro 2, Vico Equense ❶ 081 801 5668
ⓦ www.museomineralogicocampano.it ❶ 09.00–13.00, 17.00–20.00 Tues–Sat, 09.00–13.00 Sun Mar–Sept; 09.00–13.00, 16.30–19.00 Tues–Sat Oct–Feb ❶ Admission charge

Santissima Annunziata
Beautifully situated church overlooking a stunning drop to the sea below. While the original structure was built in the 14th century, numerous additions have obscured its former look.
ⓐ Via Puntamare, Vico Equense ❶ No phone ❶ 09.00–10.30 Mon–Sat, 09.00–12.30 Sun

TAKING A BREAK

Bars & cafés
Bar Villa Fondi £ Rest your feet and soak up the views from this bar situated above the Museo Georges Vallet overlooking the Bay of Naples. The gardens make it an especially choice venue on hot days when they provide ample shade. ⓐ Via Ripa di Cassano, Vico Equense
❶ 081 534 1050 ❶ 12.00–15.00, 18.30–23.00 Tues–Sun

Gelateria Latteria Gabriele £ Not just an ice cream shop, this *gelateria* is also well known for its sandwiches, cheeses and cold meats. Despite this, the *gelato* (ice cream) and *granita* (flavoured ice) combinations truly steal the show. ⓐ Corso Umberto I 5, Vico Equense ❶ 081 879 8744
❶ 09.00–14.00, 16.00–24.00 Wed–Mon; open daily July–Aug
❶ Closed 2 weeks in Jan

Restaurants
Da Gigino £ This long-established and popular pizzeria invented the term 'pizza by the metre' and continues to produce massive

⬢ *Santissima Annunziata at Vico Equense is perched over a perilous cliff*

lengths of the tasty treat every day.
ⓐ Via Nicotera 15, Vico Equense ⓣ 081 879 8309 ⓛ 12.00–01.00

Al Buco ££ Unpretentious home-style restaurant offering solid takes on local favourites, including pastas and sweet desserts. ⓐ Via Roma 26, Vico Equense ⓣ 081 801 6255 ⓛ 12.00–15.30, 19.00–23.30 Tues–Sun
ⓘ Closed 20 days in Nov

AFTER DARK

Restaurants
Antichi Sapori ££–£££ There are only 12 tables at this family-run establishment – so be sure to arrive early if you want to get one. The brothers who run the place are devoted to excellence, particularly with their wine list. In summer, meals are taken on the outdoor terrace.
ⓐ Via Bell'alba 30, Vico Equense ⓣ 081 801 6371 ⓛ 12.00–15.30, 19.00–23.00 Thur–Tues

Torre del Saracino ££–£££ Seafood is the speciality at this temple to food. If you want to try something truly special, be sure to order the fish and vegetable ravioli for which the restaurant is famous. ⓐ Via Torretta 9, Vico Equense ⓣ 081 802 8555 ⓦ www.torredelsaracino.it ⓛ 12.30–15.30, 19.30–23.30 Tues–Sat, 12.30–15.30 Sun

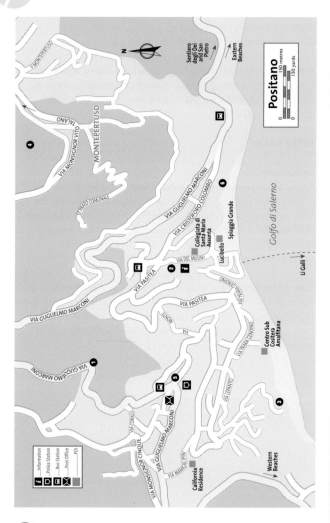

Positano

0 — 150 metres
0 — 150 yards

Golfo di Salerno

- Information
- Police Station
- Bus Station
- Post Office
- POI

Sentiero degli Dei and San Pietro

Eastern Beaches

MONTEPERTUSO

VIA MONTEPERTUSO

VIA MONSIGNOR VITO TALANO

STRADA COMUNALE

VIA GUGLIELMO MARCONI

VIA CRISTOFORO COLOMBO

Collegiata di Santa Maria Assunta

VIA DEL MULINI

VIA PASITEA

VIA GUGLIELMO MARCONI

VIA PASITEA

VIA MONTE

VIA TRARA GENOINO

VIA TRARA GENOINO

Spiaggia Grande

Lucibello

Li Galli

Centro Sub Costiera Amalfitana

VIA CORALLI

VIA GUGLIELMO MARCONI

VIA MONSIGNOR CINQUE

VIA MAMM... PIN

Western Beaches

California Residence

Positano

With the exception of Capri, Positano is probably the destination of choice for the rich and famous. Drawn to its picturesque beauty, famous names such as John Steinbeck and Pablo Picasso have been inspired by the colourful homes that cling precariously to the rock cliffs which plunge down to the harbour.

Unlike Amalfi, further along the coast, Positano does not have a long and proud history to draw from. Instead, its exposed location made it prone to numerous pirate raids throughout the years, eventually driving numerous residents away when emigration to the US made a new life more accessible.

Prices in Positano mean that package tourists rarely stay long. Rather, it attracts independently wealthy holidaymakers and is a must-see stop for drivers along the Amalfi Coast. Petite in size, it can feel decidedly packed during the summer season as hundreds of day-trippers descend on the town.

BEACHES

Eastern beaches
Three beaches lie to the east of Positano: Arienzo, Ciumicello and La Porta. Pebbles line most of the seaside stretches, but the clear waters make up for any inconvenience.
ⓐ East of Positano ❶ Deckchair rentals are available from €15 per day

Li Galli
Get away from the masses by taking a boat ride out to the archipelago known as Li Galli. According to Homer, the islands were the home of the Sirens – a group of mythical women who murdered sailors by attracting them to the rocks through their magical singing skills.
ⓐ By boat from Spiaggia Grande

◆ *Houses sweeping down to the sea in Positano*

Spiaggia Grande

Positano's main beach and centre of all the action. People-watching opportunities are excellent at this see-and-be-seen sun spot.

ⓐ Immediately next to the marina

Western beaches

Head to Fornillo using one of the regular boat services from the Marina. While the beach is a bit scrubby, the views are stunning – and the boat ride means it's often less crowded than other beaches.

ⓐ West of Positano

THINGS TO SEE & DO

Centro Sub Cositera Amalfitana (Amalfi Coast Centre of Culture)

If you're a keen scuba diver – or want to learn how to become one – then sign up for a course or rent equipment from this dive shop. You might want to think twice during the summer months when Positano's poor sanitation turns the water decidedly murky.

ⓐ Via Fornillo ⓣ 089 812 148 ⓛ Hours vary ⓘ A 2-hour dive costs approximately €60 per person

Collegiata di Santa Maria Assunta (Santa Maria Assunta College)

This 13th-century church is at the heart of the celebrations during Positano's annual Festival of the Assunta. Outside this time, it is well worth a stop to admire the majolica dome, a Byzantine icon, named the 'Black Madonna'.

ⓐ Piazza Flavio Gioia ⓣ 089 875 480 ⓦ www.chiesapositano.com
ⓛ 08.00–12.00, 16.00–19.00

Lucibello

Charter a boat at this rental shop offering small motorboats and competitive prices starting from €30 per hour.

ⓐ Spiaggia Grande ⓣ 089 875 5032 ⓛ 09.00–20.00 Apr–Nov

○ *Marina Grande and the majolica dome of Santa Maria Assunta College*

Sentiero degli Dei (Trail of the Gods)

The Amalfi Coast's most memorable hike is this trail leading from Positano to Praiano. Definitely not for novices, it can be challenging due to its precarious ridge sections and rocky, uphill climbs. As you would suspect from the name of the trail and its location, the views are worth worshipping.

ⓐ Trail begins on Via Chiesa Nuova to the right of the church

TAKING A BREAK

Bars & cafés

Il Grottino Azzurro £–££ ❶ The food is sound, but it's the wine cellar that draws the masses. Most vintages are locally produced.

ⓐ Via Guglielmo Marconi 302–304 ☎ 089 875 466 🕐 12.30–14.30, 19.30–22.30 daily ❶ Closed Wed Jan–mid-Feb

Restaurants

La Zagara £ ❷ It's a complete tourist trap, but this pizza and panini place warrants a stop. The waiting staff may apply pressure for you to eat fast depending on the season, crowds and time of day.

ⓐ Via dei Mulini 6 ☎ 089 875 964 Ⓦ www.lazagara.com
🕐 09.00–01.00 Apr–mid-Nov

Pupetto ££ ❸ Beachside restaurant based in Hotel Pupetto that has been around since Positano's earliest days as a popular resort back in the 1950s.

ⓐ Via Fornillo 37 ☎ 089 875 087 Ⓦ www.hotelpupetto.it 🕐 12.30–15.00, 19.30–22.00 ❶ Closed Nov–Mar

AFTER DARK

Restaurants

Donna Rosa ££ ❹ For an intimate evening filled with romance, book yourself into this elegant trattoria boasting views over the village.

Evenings are always packed, so if you want a last-minute table, try at lunchtime instead. ⓐ Via Montepertuso 97–99 ⓣ 089 811 806 ⓛ 18.00–23.00 daily Aug; 11.00–14.00 Wed–Mon, 19.00–23.00 daily ⓘ Closed Tues Nov–Easter

Il Capitano £££ ❺   This restaurant in Hotel Montemare is Positano's best – as agreed by residents and visitors alike. Don't go expecting anything outrageous – just classic dishes prepared perfectly. The fish and seafood options are especially good. ⓐ Via Pasitea 119 ⓣ 089 875 010 ⓦ www.hotelmontemare.it ⓛ 12.00–15.00, 19.30–22.30 Thur–Tues, 19.30–22.30 Wed ⓘ Closed Nov–Apr

Clubs
Music on the Rocks ££   ❻   Early in the evening, the soothing sounds from the piano bar draw courting couples, but as the night progresses the music gets livelier. Spread over two levels, this is a great place to kick back and let your hair down. ⓐ Via Grotto dell'Incanto 51 ⓣ 089 875 874 ⓦ www.musicontherocks.it ⓛ 22.00–early morning daily Easter–mid-Oct

Praiano

Less a town and more a collection of houses, the community of Praiano rests on one side of the Capo Sottile promontory, with Vettica Maggiore lying directly opposite. In the summer months, a drive through the town can be arduous – not only because of the sharp twists and turns, but also because of the narrow width of the road. If you are scared of heights, be sure not to look out of your side windows as you drive.

For those in the know, Praiano is considered a sort of mini-Positano complete with a postage-stamp-sized beach, small fishing cove and simple accommodation suitable for those on a budget. Vettica Maggiore has a larger beach to offer visitors along with the picturesque church of San Gennaro. Many consider the views from the church outside the square one of the highlights of a visit to the Amalfi Coast.

BEACHES

Conca dei Marini

Less a beach and more a seaside resort, this tiny village nestled in a cove was once one of the most powerful ports along the coast. Today, it is most well known as the base for explorations of the Grotta dello Smeraldo – an emerald-green cave that was discovered in 1932. From the town, it is possible to rent a boat or even swim to this colourful destination.
ⓐ Conca dei Marini

Marina di Furore

Slim strip of beach at the bottom of a steep footpath surrounded by fisherman's huts hewn carved from the rock cliffs surrounding it.
ⓐ West of Praiano reached from a viaduct above the river valley at Vallone di Furone

Marina di Praia

Small fishing community boasting a tiny beach between two rock cliffs.
ⓐ Located on a small extension to the east of Praiano

Vettica Maggiore

A small beach exists at this village located on the western side of the Capo Sotile promontory from Praiano.

ⓐ West of Praiano

THINGS TO SEE & DO

La Boa

Though not as good an option as the diving centre in Positano, this dive shop offers classes and equipment rentals at advantageous prices.

ⓐ Via Marina di Praia ☎ 089 813 034 🕑 Hours vary ❶ Closed Nov–Feb

Chiesa di San Luca (St Luke's Church)

Praiano's main church is this 16th-century structure featuring some elegant majolica tile flooring and a few minor paintings – the most notable being one by the artist Giovanni Bernardo Lama.

ⓐ Piazza San Luca ☎ 089 874 165 🕑 Hours vary

🔺 *Marina di Praia, Praiano*

Ecomuseo (Eco-Museum)

European funds have helped preserve the history of the Amalfi Coast in the form of this collection of buildings dedicated to telling the story of the coast's culture and traditions. Along with a basic restaurant, there is a paper-making museum, cinema and cultural centre worth exploring.

ⓐ Marina di Furore ❶ 089 830 781 🕐 Hours vary

Grotta dello Smeraldo (Emerald Grotto)

Capri may have the Blue Grotto, but the Amalfi Coast has its emerald-green sister. Most find Capri's offering more spectacular, but this smaller cave still gets plenty of visitors. Supposedly, it is possible to see the profile of former Italian leader Mussolini in the formation of one of the stalagmites.

ⓐ West of Conci dei Marini off the main road ❶ 089 871 107
ⓦ www.amalfitouristoffice.it 🕐 09.30–16.00 Apr–Oct; 09.00–15.00 Nov–Mar

TAKING A BREAK

Bars & cafés

Al Monazeno £ Hidden at the foot of a cliff overlooking a tiny bay, this snack bar and café is worth hunting for, if only to listen to the waves rush in. ⓐ Via Anna Magnani ❶ 349 077 2544 ⓦ www.monazeno-fiordo-furore.com 🕐 11.45–15.30, 18.30–22.30 June–Oct

Restaurants

Alfonso a Mare ££–£££ It's not the best eatery in town, but its beachside location offers plenty of inspiration. Play it safe by sticking to the seafood options on the menu. On hot days, the covered terrace is especially appreciated. ⓐ Via Marina di Praia 6 ❶ 089 874 091 🕐 12.00–15.30, 18.30–23.00 Apr–Oct

La Brace £££ The simple food – mostly regional pizzas and pastas – are uniformly excellent, but it's the stunning views that warrant the cost at this restaurant located on Praiano's main drag. ⓐ Via Gennaro Capriglione 146 ⓣ 089 874 226 ⓛ 12.00–15.00, 19.00–22.30 Thur–Tues mid-Mar–Oct

Ristorante Da Armandino £££ This relaxed beachside restaurant offers fresh dishes – many prepared with fish caught that day and unloaded on the nearby pier. The dish of the day is always a good choice. ⓐ Via Marina di Praia 1 ⓣ 089 874 087 ⓦ www.trattoriadaarmandino.it ⓛ 13.00–16.00, 19.00–24.00 Apr–Oct

AFTER DARK

Restaurants
Hostaria da Bacco ££ Typically Amalfitan cooking done with care and flair. If you're sick of seafood, this is one of the few places along the coast that also boasts an extensive menu of locally produced meats.
ⓐ Via GB Lama 9, Furore ⓣ 089 830 360 ⓦ www.baccofurore.it
ⓛ 13.00–15.30, 19.30–22.30 ⓘ Closed 2 weeks in Nov

Clubs
Africana £–££ This atmospheric bar/nightclub is situated inside an actual grotto. Popular with residents across the peninsula, it keeps going until the wee hours of the morning. During the summer, direct boats run to and from Salerno, Maiori, Minori and Amalfi. ⓐ West of Marina di Praia ⓣ 339 807 7481 ⓦ www.africananightclub.it ⓛ 21.00–04.00 ⓘ Closed Mon, Oct–May

● *Rome's Colosseum lit up at dusk*

 EXCURSIONS
Out & about

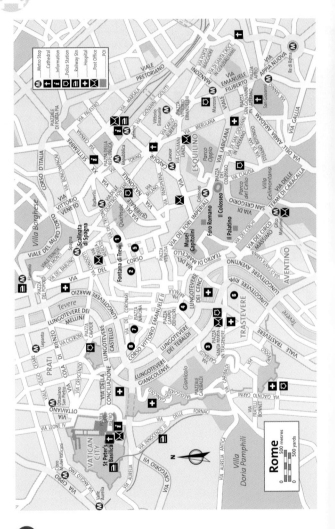

Rome

Approximately 2½ hours north of Naples is the Italian capital city of
Rome. As capital of the Roman Empire, the city's power stretched over
most of Europe and into North Africa until the Empire collapsed in
AD 476. The ruins that remain from this period are of great cultural
interest. If embarking on a day trip, must-see stops include the famed
Colosseum, site of the great gladiatorial battles of the period; St Peter's
Basilica and Vatican City, including the wondrous Sistine Chapel; and the
shopping district located around the Trevi Fountain and Spanish Steps.
If you have the time, try to give yourself an extra day or two to take in all
the sights.

THINGS TO SEE & DO

Il Colosseo (The Colosseum)

Recently elected as one of the new 'Seven Wonders of the World', the
Colosseum is a symbol of Rome and its power as an Empire. Construction
began under the orders of the Emperor Vespasian in AD 72 and after
completion it quickly became the focal point for gladiatorial exhibitions.
ⓐ Piazza del Colosseo ❶ 06 700 5469 ⓦ www.pierreci.it
🕐 08.30–18.15 ❶ Admission charge

Fontana di Trevi (Trevi Fountain)

You may not be able to follow Anita Ekberg into the waters any more,
but the Trevi Fountain is still one of the highlights of the city. Built in 1732
by Pope Clement, it is now said that if you throw a coin into the fountain,
you will return to Rome one day.
ⓐ Piazza di Trevi

Foro Romano (Roman Forum)

From the 2nd to 4th centuries AD, the Forum became a symbol of power
as construction on a number of temples, buildings and courts
transformed the square into the heart of the Empire.

ⓐ Entrances located on Via Sacra, Via di San Teodoro, Via dei Fori Imperiali and Via Foro Romano ❶ 06 700 5469 ⓛ 08.30–18.15 Apr–Sept; 08.30–16.30 Oct–Mar

Musei Capitolini (Capitoline Museum)

This museum, founded in 1471 by Pope Sixtus IV, is the oldest public art gallery in the world. Housed in two palaces on the piazza del Campidoglio, the collection boasts numerous masterpieces from the Renaissance period, including works by Tintoretto, Caravaggio and Titian.
ⓐ Piazza del Campidoglio 1 ❶ 06 8205 9127 ⓦ www.museicapitolini.org
ⓛ 09.00–20.00 closed Mon ❶ Admission charge

Il Palatino (The Palatine)

It is believed that the area known as Il Palatino was the site of the original settlement of Rome founded by Romulus and Remus. During the height of the Empire, it became the preferred residence for the rich and

● *View down over Piazza San Pietro from the top of St Peter's Basilica*

élite – many imperial residences were built on the site making it the most expensive address in the world.

ⓐ Via di San Gregorio 30 ⓣ 063 996 7700 ⓛ 08.30–sunset
ⓘ Admission charge

Scalinata di Spagna (Spanish Steps)

Named for the Spanish Embassy to the Vatican that was once located close by, the Spanish Steps, completed in 1729, are an elegant set of steps that lead from the church of Trinità dei Monti to the streets of Rome's designer district made up of the vias Condotti, Borgognona and Frattina.

ⓐ Scalinata di Trinità dei Monti

Vatican City & St Peter's Basilica

You could spend days in the Vatican and not even scratch the surface of what is arguably one of the most fascinating cities on the planet. Surrounded by, but a separate nation from, Rome, the Vatican is the capital of the Roman Catholic faith, with St Peter's Basilica the focal point. On major religious days, the pope addresses believers from the square (Piazza San Pietro) immediately outside the church. While in the Vatican, be sure to see the Vatican Museums, famous as home to Michelangelo's Sistine Chapel. Dress appropriately for your visit: those wearing shorts, uncovered shoulders or short skirts will be turned away.

Vatican Museum ⓐ Viale del Vaticano ⓣ 06 6988 3333
ⓦ www.vatican.va ⓛ 09.45–16.45 Sat Mar–Oct; 08.45–13.45 Mon–Sat
Nov–Feb ⓘ Closed Catholic holidays. Admission charge except free last
Sun of every month, but no guided tours

St Peter's Basilica ⓐ Viale del Vaticano ⓛ 07.00–19.00 Apr–Sept;
07.00–18.00 Oct–Mar

TAKING A BREAK

Bars & cafés

Il Gelato di San Crispino £ ❶ The best ice cream in town. Flavours
evolve according to the season with summer focusing on fresh

berries and citrus tastes, and winter boasting toffees, chocolates and late-season fruits such as plums. ⓐ Via della Panettaria 42 ⓣ 06 679 3924 ⓛ 12.00–01.00 daily Mar–Sept; 12.00–00.30 Wed–Mon Oct–Feb

La Caffettiera £–££ ❷ Mix with the big boys at this favourite café for politicians and power-players. The coffee at this place truly has a kick to it. ⓐ Piazza di Pietra 65 ⓣ 06 679 8147 ⓦ www.lacaffettieraonline.com ⓛ 07.00–21.00 Mon–Sat, 08.00–21.00 Sun

Enoteca Ferrara ££ ❸ Tapas-style dishes are served with flair in this Italian version of a gastropub. The wine list is extensive, yet pricey. If you're in a hurry, it's possible to pick up nibbles from the in-house deli to take with you. ⓐ Piazza Trilussa ⓣ 06 5833 3920 ⓛ Restaurant: 20.00–23.30, Tapas bar: 18.00–02.00

Restaurants

Da Michele £ ❹ Kosher pizza? That's right! This convenient pizza parlour situated near the Trevi Fountain has a menu of over 40 varieties, all dairy-free – so you won't find a speck of cheese on any of them. Great for the lactose-intolerant. ⓐ Via dell'Umiltà 31 ⓣ 349 252 5347 ⓛ 08.00–22.00 Sun–Fri Apr–Sept; 08.00–18.00 Sun–Fri Oct–Mar ❶ Closed Jewish holidays

Bruschetteria degli Angeli £–££ ❺ Bar-style eatery with tables that overlook a small park. The speciality of the house is *bruschetta* topped with pretty much anything you might desire. Pastas and meat dishes are also on offer. ⓐ Piazza B Cairoli 2A ⓣ 06 6880 5789 ⓛ 12.30–15.30, 19.30–01.30

Le Mani in Pasta £–££ ❻ Home-style cuisine done very well. For those on a budget, you can't beat the great pasta dishes and well-cooked meat selections at this unassuming little trattoria. ⓐ Via dei Genovesi 37 ⓣ 06 581 6017 ⓛ 12.30–15.00, 19.30–23.30 Tues–Sun

Il Fico ££ ❼   Fine dining in friendly surroundings. Only fresh seasonal vegetables are used – try the terrine of stuffed zucchini flowers or eggplant with mozzarella di bufala. ⓐ Via di Monte Giordano 49 ❶ 06 687 5568 ⓦ www.ilfico.com ⓛ 12.00–24.00 daily

L'Altro Mastai £££ ❽   Considered one of the finest restaurants in Rome, this Italian eatery offers great, seasonal dishes in an atmosphere of perfect refinement. The place to go if you want to splurge. Reservations are essential. ⓐ Via Giraud 53 ❶ 06 6830 1296 ⓛ 19.30–23.30 Tues–Sat ❶ Closed Aug

🔺 *Restaurant at a pavement café by the Pantheon*

Herculaneum & Vesuvius

The town of Herculaneum thought it got off lightly during the eruption of Vesuvius in AD 79, only to find that a change in the winds sealed the city's fate. When the lava and ash changed direction, residents were caught unexpectedly and buried under tonnes of earth – essentially sealed away forever.

Unlike Pompeii, which was never dramatically resettled after the disaster, Herculaneum thrived once again and is today one of the most densely populated regions in Italy. The town also serves as the main gateway to the deadly – and still highly active – volcano, and coach tours and hikes depart Herculaneum to scale its heights.

● *Excavated mosaic in the House of Neptune and Amphitrite at Herculaneum*

THINGS TO SEE & DO

Cratere del Vesuvio (Mount Vesuvius)

Still active after all these years, Mount Vesuvius is both the bane of Campania and the source of all its success. Despite its ever-present threat, locals owe much to this volcano – especially farmers – as the volcanic soil has made the area incredibly lush and fruitful. Without it, many of the crops and farms that exist today would not be there.

A hike up Vesuvius is a popular day trip and easy to do even if you aren't a regular walker. Over 200,000 visitors make the climb each year and you are allowed to go as far as the rim of the cone, just 200 m (218 yds) from the surface of the crater. The best time of year to attempt a hike is during May and June when weather conditions are favourable.

ⓐ Cratere del Vesuvio ❶ 081 771 0939 ❶ 09.00–2 hours before sunset

Scavi di Ercolano (Herculaneum Excavation)

Once a desired residence, the town of Herculaneum has hit hard times over the past two millennia since the original Roman city was destroyed. Today, Herculaneum is one of the most densely populated and poorest communities in Europe – so be sure to hold on to your wallet when travelling through the streets.

Less visited than Pompeii, but no less fascinating, Herculaneum (or Ercolano as it is now known) was the town of choice for Rome's élite. Residents thought they had escaped Vesuvius's wrath in AD 79 until the change in the wind resulted in their demise. After years of construction on top of the site, it is thought that only a fraction of its treasures have been unearthed.

ⓐ Corso Resina 6 ❶ 081 732 4338 ⓦ www.pompeiisites.org
❶ 08.30–19.30, ticket office closes 18.00 Apr–Oct; 08.30–17.00, ticket office closes 15.30 Nov–Mar

⬥ *The volcanic backdrop to Naples' cityscape*

TAKING A BREAK

Bars & cafés
Italia Caffe & Pasticceria £ Refreshing ices, strong cups of coffee and pastries that will satisfy any sweet tooth – it's all here. 🅰 Corso Italia 17 🕿 081 732 1499 🕐 07.30–20.30 Mon–Sat, 07.30–14.30 Sun

Restaurants
La Fornacella £ Located in a less than salubrious locale, this restaurant caters heavily for the tourist trade with simple dishes made fast. Luckily, the results are pretty tasty. 🅰 Via IV Novembre 90–92 🕿 081 777 4861 🔘 www.lafornacellasrl.it 🕐 08.00–24.00 Tues–Sun

For fine dining, Herculaneum is not recommended. Instead, head over to the nearby seaside resort of **Torre del Greco** for more enticing offerings. Some of the better establishments include:

Gaetano a Mare £–££ A favourite with locals for many years, this relaxed restaurant offers strong takes on traditional dishes. When ordering the catch of the day, be sure to specify the way you like it cooked – be it fried, baked or grilled. 🅰 Via Litoranea 5, Torre del Greco 🕿 081 883 1558 🕐 12.00–15.00, 19.30–23.00 Sat–Thur

Ristorante Pernice Salvatore ££ Elegant eatery offering both indoor and outdoor seating areas. The seasonal menu changes regularly. When in doubt, order the catch of the day. 🅰 Via Ruggiero 45, Torre del Greco 🕿 081 883 2297 🕐 12.00–15.00, 10.30–23.00

Pompeii

If you make one pilgrimage during your time on the Neapolitan Riviera, choose Pompeii. A bustling town of trade and holiday destination for the privileged of the Roman Empire, it disappeared off the face of the earth following the eruption of Mount Vesuvius in AD 79.

Today, this UNESCO World Heritage Site is one of the main draws for visitors to the region, attracted by the glorious frescoes, restored villas and temples that give a glimpse into what life was like during the Roman age. Give yourself a minimum of three hours to explore the site fully.

🔺 *Plaster-cast of a victim at Pompeii*

THINGS TO SEE & DO

Scavi di Pompeii (Pompeii Excavation)

It's a myth that the ruins of Pompeii have only been attracting tourists in modern times. Locals have been aware of this UNESCO World Heritage Site for centuries – but it wasn't until 1750 that visitors began to arrive in droves … and they still do. Even on the coldest days, this finely preserved collection of Roman ruins is packed with tourists.

Pompeii was literally petrified in time during the eruption of Mount Vesuvius in AD 79 when thousands of tonnes of volcanic ash and pumice buried the buildings and its residents alive. Despite the numerous warning signs that a disaster was about to occur – including regular earthquakes and plumes of smoke – many locals assumed that they could weather the disaster, and their bodies remain a testament to their foolishness. Some of the more grisly sights are the plaster casts that were made from the voids that people's frames made under the layers of earth. The defensive poses show how fast the disaster overtook them and the fear they must have experienced while they were buried alive.

There are numerous highlights to any visit, with particular note being given to the Casa del Fauno with its paintings and mosaics, the frescoes of the Villa dei Misteri and the imposing structure of the Forum.

Give yourself plenty of time to explore – at least three hours – and try to avoid holidays and weekends when the crowds can be overpowering. Children and the elderly should also avoid going on very hot days as there is little shade available. Wear a hat, plenty of sunscreen and carry bottles of water when you go inside.

ⓐ Via Villa dei Misteri 2 ⓣ 081 857 5347 ⓦ www.pompeiisites.org
ⓛ 08.30–19.30 (ticket office closes 18.00) Apr–Oct; 08.30–17.00 (ticket office closes 15.30) Nov–Mar

⬥ Remnants of the ancient ruined city of Pompeii

TAKING A BREAK

Restaurants

Zi Caterina £ In this touristy area, it's refreshing to find a restaurant that's both cheap and tasty. Locals are regular customers – always a good sign. ⓐ Via Roma 20 ⓣ 081 850 7447 ⓦ www.zicaterina.it ⓛ 12.00–23.30

Lucullus £–££ In honour of the gods, this restaurant has been decorated in an eclectic manner complete with swaying palm trees and faux-marble busts. While this might put you off entering, the *antipasti* (appetisers) buffet is a good choice for those looking for variety. ⓐ Via Plinio 129 ⓣ 081 861 3055 ⓛ 12.00–15.00, 19.00–23.00 Wed–Mon

Ristorante President ££–£££ Very traditional establishment with formal waiters and a seafood-focused menu. Be sure to leave room for the delicious homemade desserts. ⓐ Piazza Schettino 12 ⓣ 081 850 7245 ⓛ 12.00–15.00, 19.30–23.30 Tues–Sat, 12.00–15.00 Sun ⓘ Closed Christmas and 2 weeks in Aug

Il Principe £££ Ever wondered what the Romans might have eaten? Now is your chance to find out. In addition to Neapolitan favourites, this atmospheric dining spot serves up intriguing dishes derived from ancient Roman recipes. ⓐ Piazza Bartolo Longo 8 ⓣ 081 850 5566 ⓦ www.ilprincipe.com ⓛ 12.30–15.00, 20.00–23.00 Tues–Sat, 12.30–15.00 Sun

EXCURSIONS

Amalfi

Back in the 11th century, Naples was a mere village when compared to the might of the maritime republic of Amalfi. The city, blessed with a naturally deep port and hidden in the fold of the cliffs of the coast, made it easily defensible. Yet the lack of land in which to spread out eventually resulted in its downfall. After its loss of power following the plague of 1348, it remained untouched until 19th-century travellers rediscovered the charms of this once-great community.

THINGS TO SEE & DO

Duomo di Amalfi (Amalfi Cathedral)
Dating back to the 9th century, this cathedral is the focal point for the town, boasting architecture from a variety of periods. Don't miss the Cappella del Crocefisso – the only remaining part existing of the original structure.
ⓐ Piazza del Duomo ① 089 871 059 ⓛ 09.00–19.00 Apr–June; 09.00–21.00 July–Sept; 09.30–17.15 Oct & Mar; 10.00–13.00, 14.30–16.30 Nov–Feb ① Admission charge for Cappella only

Museo della Carta (Paper Museum)
Explore the regional tradition of paper-making at this museum showcasing the artistry and techniques required for the production of luxurious, handmade stationery.
ⓐ Palazzo Pagliara, Via delle Cartiere 23 ① 089 830 4561
ⓦ www.museodellacarta.it ⓛ 10.00–18.00 Apr–June & Oct; 10.00–20.00 July–Sept; 10.00–15.00 Tues–Sun Nov–Mar ① Admission charge

TAKING A BREAK

Bars & cafés
Bar Risacca £ Join the locals at this relaxed drinking spot and watch people going about their daily business. ⓐ Piazza Umberto I 16

● *The busy streets of Amalfi*

🕿 089 872 866 🌐 www.risacca.com 🕐 08.00–02.00 Apr–Oct; 08.00–13.30, 15.30–24.00 Tues–Sun Nov–Mar

Gran Caffe di Amalfi £ Enjoy an espresso or aperitif at this elegant café boasting incredible sea views. 🅰 Corso delle Repubbliche Marinare 37 🕿 089 871 047 🕐 07.00–22.00 Tues–Sun 🛇 Closed Nov–Jan

Restaurants
Da Maria £–££ There are plenty of pizzerias to choose from in Amalfi, but this is the best of the bunch. 🅰 Via Lorenzo d'Amalfi 14 🕿 089 871 880 🕐 12.00–15.00, 19.00–23.30 Tues–Sun June–Sept daily 🛇 Closed Nov

Da Gemma ££ If children are in tow, then head straight to this popular establishment that has been serving tasty meals to patrons for over a century. Fancy enough to impress you, yet casual enough to make children comfy, it's a relief for parents looking for affordable Neopolitan cuisine that doesn't shirk on quality. 🅰 Via Fra Gerardo Sasso 9 🕿 089 871 345 🕐 12.30–14.45, 20.00–23.00 Thur–Tues

La Caravella £££ By far the best restaurant in town. 🅰 Via Matteo Camera 12 🕿 089 871 029 🕐 12.00–14.30, 19.30–22.30 Wed–Mon 🌐 www.ristorantelacaravella.it 🛇 Closed mid-Nov–Dec

AFTER DARK

Bars & restaurants
Cantina San Nicola £–££ Fantastic wine bar with a large selection of vintages in all price ranges. 🅰 Salita Marino Sebaste 8 🕿 089 830 4549 🕐 12.00–14.30, 18.00–late Mon–Sat

Lido Azzurro ££ The seaside location makes this unpretentious eatery popular with tourists. Go for the simple pasta and fish dishes prepared fresh every day. 🅰 Lungomare dei Cavaliere 5 🕿 089 871 384 🕐 12.30–15.00, 19.30–23.00 Tues–Sun Mar–Dec 🛇 Closed Jan–Feb

Salerno

Founded by the Romans back in 194 BC, the town of Salerno
(or Salernum as it was then known) became a superpower in the region
when the Normans made it their capital in AD 1077. For three centuries,
fortune favoured the metropolis, leaving behind a collection of beautiful
Romanesque buildings worthy of modern-day exploration. Regular train
services on the Calabria line from Naples's Stazione Centrale (Central
Station) make a trip here possible in less than 45 minutes.

THINGS TO SEE & DO

Duomo (Cathedral)
Built in honour of the town's patron saint, St Matthew, Salerno's
cathedral is designed in the Romanesque style, with baroque finishings
added during the 18th century.
ⓐ Piazza Alfano 1 ⓣ 089 231 387 ⓛ 07.30–20.00

◭ *Salerno Cathedral*

Museo Archeologico Provinciale (Provincial Archaeology Museum)

Explore the history of the town in this museum housed in a former abbey. The highlight of the collection is a 1st-century bust of Apollo made from bronze.

🄰 Via San Benedetto 28 ☎ 089 231 135 🕒 09.30–19.30 Tues–Sat, 09.00–13.00 Sun

Pinoteca Provinciale (Provincial History Museum)

Housed in a 17th-century palazzo (palace), this collection of paintings dating from the 15th–18th centuries was pieced together from finds housed in abandoned churches and buildings in the region.

🄰 Via Mercanti 62 ☎ 089 258 3073 🕒 09.00–20.00 Tues–Sun

TAKING A BREAK

Restaurants

Trattoria Pizzeria Zi Renato £ Great pizza served in typically Italian surroundings – right down to the candles in Chianti bottles and red-and-white checked tablecloths.

🄰 Via Roma 170 ☎ 089 228 018 🆆 www.zirenato.it 🕒 12.30–15.30, 19.30–23.45 🛇 Closed Tues

Cenacolo ££ Located across the street from the Duomo, this eatery is probably the best in town – although the competition isn't exactly strong. Regional flavours and products are always highlighted.

🄰 Piazza Alfano I 4 ☎ 089 238 818 🕒 12.30–15.00, 19.30–23.00 Tues–Sat, 12.30–15.00 Sun 🛇 Closed 3 weeks in Aug

---

▶ *Via Nazario Sauro, Naples*

LIFESTYLE
Italian life

Food & drink

SERVICE & ORDERING

As meals along the Neapolitan Riviera are a relaxed affair, service in the region tends to be slow. It's not that the waiters are trying to avoid or offend you – they're just used to a slower pace and way of eating. While most restaurants do have menus, they often do not have English translations available. Try to order one of the specials of the day to ensure your meal uses only the freshest of ingredients – usually picked up that morning by the chef in the local markets.

ALCOHOLIC BEVERAGES

Campania has been producing wine ever since the Greeks introduced grape cultivation to the region back in 800 BC. While local vintages aren't as famous as the wines produced in the north of the country, there are still plenty worth hunting – both red and white. Varieties to look out for include the reds and rosés of Castel San Lorenzo in Salerno, the Amalfi Coast's Furore, Tramonti and Ravello, and Lacrima Christi (Tears of Christ) produced using the volcanic soil of Mount Vesuvius.

● Local produce is best

Liqueurs are another speciality of the Neapolitan Riviera, especially *limoncello* made from the lemons of Capri and the Amalfi Coast, the digestive *finocchietto* produced from wild fennel, and *nanassino* produced from prickly pears.

BREAKFAST

Breakfast is a simple affair usually involving a cup of coffee and a fresh pastry or selection of breads. Local cafés usually have an ample supply of fresh baked goods available for consumption, with residents including a stop at their local coffee shop for a quick bite and a newspaper read on their way to work.

DESSERTS & SWEETS

Neapolitans certainly do have a sweet tooth. Whether it be a cone of *gelato* (ice cream) or a sticky pastry, they'll happily dive right in at every opportunity. Every town in Campania has a local pastry speciality, with many on the Amalfi Coast using lemon as the base of the flavouring – another example of drawing from the finest local, seasonal produce. Sweet ricotta is often used as a filling for pastries, including in the popular *pastiera* cake served in Naples as part of Easter celebrations.

In Sorrento, sample *dolcezze al limone*, a lemon pastry variety stuffed with lemon-flavoured cream.

LOCAL FOOD

The cuisine of Naples is celebrated throughout Italy and beyond due to its adherence to the practice of only using seasonal, locally grown ingredients. Ingredients used here are bursting with flavour, often grown just a few steps from where they are prepared.

While there are a number of specialities produced in Campania, some of the more noted items include:

Lemons & their by-products

Everyone is familiar with the sweet liqueur made from the rind of local lemons called *limoncello*. A staple of the region, it was originally made on the island of Capri as a dessert liqueur and remains one of the most popular souvenir purchases for visitors. Another item to keep an eye out for is honey infused with the flavours of the lemon flower for a distinctly sweet, yet tart experience.

Mozzarella

To find the best Campanian mozzarella, try to find a shop that serves as an outlet for a local farm – known as a *caseificio*. The finest quality versions of the cheese are usually found inland from the coast, but a good deli should be able to offer a delicious variety or two. When in doubt, make sure the cheese is handmade and not mass produced, to ensure flavour and quality.

Olive oil

Chefs adore the olive oil grown on the Sorrentine Peninsula, valuing its subtle sweetness – a quality infused by the volcanic soil from which it grows. It is believed that some of the groves of the region date back to the days of the Greek Empire.

Pasta di Gragano

The pasta of the Neapolitan Riviera has been a staple of local cuisine since the 16th century. Locally produced varieties exclusively use durum wheat and are naturally dried. It is believed that the quality of the air gives the variety a sweetness and fragrance that is unique.

Tomatoes

No one can match the sheer number of varieties and vine-ripened flavours of tomatoes in the Neapolitan Riviera. Each town has a native variety it is proud of, with distinctive characteristics in terms of shape, colour and size. Eat them whole to experience the overwhelming taste.

MAIN DISHES & EATING HABITS

While meat is available on the menus of the Neapolitan Riviera, most avoid these dishes in favour of the speciality of the region – seafood. The best main courses (*secondi*) draw from the catches of the area, specifically in the form of shrimp, squid, clams and dozens of fish varieties. Meals can be as simple as a flavoursome fish stew or a delicious mixed platter of fried seafood (*frittura*).

Traditionally, the main course is served following the consumption of *antipasti* – usually a plate of regional meats, cheese or vegetables – and a *primi* (first) course of pasta or soup. Due to the sheer volume of food, dinner is often an all-night affair and you will rarely be rushed unless you are eating at a restaurant that caters specifically to the tourist crowd.

Diners tend to dress up when dining out in Campania. A light suit or jacket is advisable for men, especially if you are booked into a more traditional fine dining establishment. When in doubt, avoid jeans and shorts and choose a more 'smart casual' outfit.

If you're looking for anything other than Italian specialities, you may be out of luck, especially outside Naples. The region is one of the most ethnically homogeneous in Europe and does not readily offer samples of international cuisine. However, you're unlikely to be disappointed as flavours are incredibly diverse throughout the Riviera.

Pizza

Naples claims to be the location where pizza was invented and there are plenty of locations where you can try the local dish. If you are used to deep-dish varieties or cheese-laden slices, you may be in for a surprise because local versions are more focused on the quality of the dough and tomato base. Often cheese is an optional ingredient.

The two most common types of pizza served in Naples are the pizza Romana (or Napoletana), which is a simple pizza of marinara sauce on a crisp base, and the pizza Margherita, which features the colours of the Italian flag: green for basil, white for mozzarella and red for tomatoes.

Vegetarian options

Due to the volume of fresh fruits and vegetables available in Campania, vegetarians should have no problem sating their appetites during their stay. When in doubt, stick to pasta dishes and pizzas. Many items that state they are vegetarian involve meat stocks or *pancetta* (pork). Ask your waiter for a full description of ingredients to avoid disappointment.

Menu decoder

MEATS, CHEESES, SEAFOOD AND VEGETABLES
(*Carne, formaggi, frutti di mare* and *verdure*)

Acqua pazza Light broth flavoured with herbs, often used to cook fish

Agnello Grilled or baked lamb

Aragosta Lobster

Baccalà Stew made from salted codfish

Brasato Braised beef cooked in a white wine sauce with vegetables

Carciofi Artichokes

Cassuola Casserole dish made from terracotta. Also refers to the stew cooked in the pot of the same name

Coniglio alla cacciatora Rabbit prepared in a sauce of olives, herbs and white wine

Cozze Mussels

Fagioli Beans

Fiordilatte Inferior (yet still tasty) form of mozzarella made from cow's milk instead of buffalo's milk

Frittura Seafood stir-fry, Italian-style

Frutti di mare Seafood

Involtini Choice of beef, aubergines, veal, pork or courgettes sliced thinly, stuffed and lightly fried – usually served in a tomato sauce

Melanzane Aubergines

Mozzarella di bufala Unfermented cheese made from buffalo's milk and native to the region

Parmigiano Hard yellow cheese, often grated over soups or pastas

Peperoni Multicoloured sweet peppers

Pesce al cartoccio Seasoned fish cooked in a paper envelope

Pesce spada Swordfish

Polpetti Squid

Polpo Octopus

Seppia Cuttlefish

Sogliola Sole

ANTIPASTI AND SOUP (*Zuppa*) VARIETIES

Antipasti The first dish of every meal, often consisting of deli meats, marinated vegetables or plates of seafood

Antipasti di mare Seafood selection

Antipasti misti Mixed plate of cold meats, cheeses and olives

Bruschetta Coarse slices of bread topped with olive oil, garlic and (sometimes) tomatoes

Caprese Salad of tomatoes and mozzarella drizzled with olive oil

Carpaccio Raw beef cut into thin slices and seasoned with herbed olive oil

Fragaglie Deep-fried, often breaded small fish

Fresella Country-style bread served up as part of a salad made from basil, olive oil and tomatoes

Insalata di mare Seafood salad

Minestra maritata Hearty pork soup with vegetables

Minestrone Vegetable soup with grated Parmesan cheese, often including pasta

Prosciutto e fichi Parma ham with figs

Soute di vongole Fried clams

PASTA VARIETIES AND SAUCES

Al nero di sepia In squid ink

Alla Genovese With onion and veal sauce

Alla Siciliana with a sauce of aubergines, mozzarella and basil

Alle vongole Cooked with clams

Bucatini Thick, hollow pasta variety

Cannelloni Stuffed pasta tubes, usually filled with meat or cheese

Fusilli Spiral-shaped pasta

Gnocchi Potato or semolina dumplings, usually in a tomato sauce

Ragu Tomato and meat mince sauce (usually beef)

Spaghetti Round, thin pasta

Tagliatelle Flat egg noodles

Tortelli Dumplings filled with ricotta or meat

Vermicelli Extremely thin spaghetti variety

PIZZA VARIETIES

Calzone Stuffed pizza dough, usually filled with ham and cheese. Can be baked or fried

Caprese Cherry tomatoes and mozzarella with optional rocket

Capricciosa Black olives, ham and artichoke hearts

Margherita Tomatoes, mozzarella and basil

Prosciutto crudo e rucola in bianco Rocket, mozzarella and Parma ham in a white sauce

Ripieno Folded pizza stuffed with ricotta, mozzarella, salami, basil and tomato

Ripieno fritto As above, only deep fried and sometimes stuffed with slices of pig fat

Romana/Napoletana/ Marinara Simple pizza with tomatoes, garlic, olive oil and oregano – no cheese

Salsiccia e friarielli Greens, sausage and mozzarella

SIDE DISHES (*Contorni*)
Friarelli Vegetable side dish made from broccoli fried in olive oil with garlic and red peppers

Frittata Italian-style omelette

Risotto Italian rice, often cooked in wine and mixed with seafood, meat or vegetables

Sartu Baked rice 'bowl' filled with meatballs, mozzarella and sausages

Scapece Courgettes and aubergines lightly fried and then seasoned with vinegar and mint

DESSERTS (*Dolce*)
Baba Rum-drenched cake served with cream

Gelateria Ice cream parlour

Gelato Ice cream

Granita Flavoured ice, often served with coffee

Panna Heavy cream

Pastiera Traditional Easter pie made from sweet cheese and candied orange peel

Sfogliatella Flaky pastry stuffed with sweet cheese

Shopping

Unlike cities such as Rome and Milan, Naples and the surrounding region isn't noted for its adherence to designer fashion. That's not to say that residents aren't chic; rather, it has never boasted a tradition of couture or clothes-making. The irony of this is that the northern factories producing designer duds are usually staffed with seamstresses and tailors from the south – specifically Naples.

You will find designer boutiques in Naples (around Chiaia and the Via Toledo) and on the island of Capri, but they will have limited stock as the truly fashionable are more likely do their big shopping a couple of hours away in Rome.

When shopping, it is customary for shop assistants to leave you alone, almost to the point of rudeness. Most stock is locked away in drawers, so you will have to call on them at some point if you have plans to make a purchase.

If you aren't a clothes horse, there are plenty of other wares to admire along the coast, with Naples offering the best variety. Almost every town has a market day of some sort – always a good day to make regional food purchases you plan to take back home. Just be aware that market food is fresh (no preservatives), and will go off quickly during a long journey.

SHOPPING AREAS

For high-end designer goods and local art galleries, shop in the Chiaia region of Naples. Located between Vomero and the waterfront, it is definitely the preferred neighbourhood for the rich and powerful. Capri and Positano also have high-end goods, but with much less stock available, and these shops will only open during the high season. Resort wear will be the key focus rather than everyday goods from the designer collections.

For the Neapolitan Riviera's version of the high street, go to the Via Toledo in Naples or Corso Italia in Sorrento. In addition to the local branch of the Italian department store La Rinascente (in Naples only), you will find shops like Benetton and other familiar brands. You will also find the elegant Galleria Umberto, a collection of unique boutiques under a glass and iron roof.

The Centro Storico (Old Town) of Naples is the place to head for antiquarian books, antiques and beautiful jewellery. Every piece will be unique in this part of town, so if you like what you see then chances are you won't find it anywhere else.

MARKETS

Almost every town in the Neapolitan Riviera has a market day or square; however, these are aimed purely at locals. The bulk of the goods on offer will be everyday household items or fresh foods such as cheeses, meats and sweets. For true variety, stick to the markets of Naples. Recommended stops include the antique market known as the Fiera Antiquaria Napoletana on the Villa Comunale in Chiaia (held on the last Sunday of the month), the Mercatino di Poggioreale on Via M di Caramanico for shoes (every day except Tuesday), or the fake designer-goods paradise of the Mercatino di Posillipo on Viale Virgilio in Posillipo (every Thursday). The Mercatino di Resina in Herculaneum is a great place to go for a morning if you want something truly unique as it's the largest flea market on the coast (held daily except during August).

When shopping in the markets, keep your eye on your purchases and purses at all times as markets are often a prime location for pickpocketing and petty theft. Also be aware that few stalls accept credit cards, so a supply of ready cash is advisable.

SOUVENIRS

There are heaps of things to buy along the Neapolitan Riviera, but some items make better souvenirs than others. One of the most popular purchases is a bottle of *limoncello* – the neon-yellow liqueur found in towns and shops all along the coast. The island of Capri claims to be the location where the tipple was first introduced, but the villages of the Amalfi Coast also make good varieties. Whatever you do, don't wait to make your purchase from the airport duty-free shop. Not only will the

⬤ *Porta Nolana market, Naples*

varieties be vastly inferior, they will also be more expensive. Other liqueurs made from fennel and prickly pears are available, but these are less popular with visitors' taste buds.

If you find liqueurs sickly sweet, the Neapolitan Riviera is known for the quality of its wines. Most vintages are intended to be drunk very soon after bottling, so it is not recommended that you keep it tucked away in your wine rack at home for extended periods. Wines produced here work well with seafood and fish due to the traditional cuisine of the Campanian coast.

Positano is the place to go for unique resort wear, produced in the village. It has been known as a place for quality clothing since the 1950s, although its reputation is slowly waning.

For original stationery and paper goods, Amalfi is the place to go. Paper-making has been a tradition here for centuries, and the quality of the items produced will make you want to avoid email for the rest of your life.

Finally, the town of Sorrento has a long tradition producing furniture, specifically intricate marquetry work known as *intarsio*. The better shops will be able to ship larger pieces back home to you for a reasonable price.

🔺 *Italian ceramics make a good souvenir*

Children

Neapolitans love children – of every shape, size, variety and attitude. Neapolitans are very family-orientated people and dote on children as much as they can. Often, if you are with children during your visit, you will be offered seats on public transport and strangers will come up to ruffle the hair of your little one.

Despite this love affair with children, there are few diversions along the Neapolitan Riviera for youngsters. Naples is, after all, a city where you can still see neighbourhood kids amusing themselves for hours with a ball. Not for this city the trappings of the computer-game generation. However, there are a few parks dotted around the city where little ones can let off steam.

BEACHES

When you need a break, the beach is your best bet. Try to avoid the city beaches of Naples as they tend to be badly maintained with poor water quality. Instead, the islands of Ischia, Procida and Capri or the Amalfi Coast offer better options. Unfortunately, sand beaches can be a rare find in the region, and what sand beaches there are can be extremely crowded, especially during the summer months and on weekends. Rocky outcrops can be common, lifeguards are few and the undertow is particularly strong, so make sure you either watch or accompany your little ones at all times.

EDENLANDIA

Similar to a revolving carnival, the Edenlandia funfair is an amusement park that is definitely past its prime. Rides are old and very traditional, meaning that older kids and teenagers may find the offerings distinctly unimpressive. Despite this, it's a great place to have a bit of fun.
ⓐ Viale Kennedy, Fuorigrotta ❶ 081 239 4800 🕑 14.00–20.00 Tues–Fri, 10.30–24.00 Sat & Sun Apr & May; 17.00–24.00 Mon–Fri, 10.30–24.00 Sat & Sun June & Sept; 17.00–24.00 Mon–Sat, 10.30–24.00 Sun July & Aug; 10.30–24.00 Sat & Sun Oct–Mar ❶ Admission charge

MUSEUMS & HISTORIC SIGHTS

While museums and archaeological sites are one of the draws of Naples, you would be well advised to plan your visit in advance. A trip to Pompeii can be a nightmare, especially on hot days when the baking sun and lack of shade can create havoc for families. Kids will find the ancient ruins fascinating – for a while – but it would be best for their patience levels and your state of mind to map your route through the ruins in order to save time. Locations that are of particular interest include the Museo Archeologico in Naples (see page 18), Capri's Blue Grotto (see page 37), the Castel dell'Ovo (see page 15), bubbling Mount Vesuvius (see page 75), and the ruins at Pompeii and Herculaneum (see pages 78 & 74).

BEFORE YOU GO & DURING YOUR STAY

As the Neopolitan Riviera can get both crowded and extremely hot, it can quickly become a nightmare destination for visiting families. Chaotic traffic and poorly laid pavements can cause havoc – especially if your kids are the type who like to run into the path of oncoming traffic. In order to ensure your holiday remains trouble-free, it pays to do some advance planning before you arrive in the region.

Family activities and performances are frequently offered in the Riviera. Either check for details on an events website such as ⓦ www.whatonwhen.com or call the Tourist Information offices in advance to see if something is going on during your stay. Also, be sure to bring a copy of your child's passport as proof of age with you whenever you explore the sights or take public transport, as many establishments will provide a discount for under-12s.

The key to success when visiting the Neopolitan Riviera is to find a base that combines a convenient location with a wealth of facilities. Children like things to do – so you may have to wait to stay in that beautiful boutique property packed with antique goodies in favour of a concrete block that boasts a swimming pool and buffet restaurant. During school holiday periods and the busy summer months, you will need to book well in advance to make sure you snag the property that best suits your needs.

Mediterranean families are pretty flexible when it comes to bedtime. Seeing kids running around café tables at midnight is not uncommon as the idea of hiring a babysitter would never be considered by a Neapolitan mother. If you want a romantic night out away from the children, you will have to search long and hard for a sitter service. Choose to either bring the children with you or splash out on a five-star resort that truly offers everything you could imagine – including on-site babysitters.

Baby formula milk and nappies can be purchased at most chemists (*farmacie*) and supermarkets; however, finding ordinary milk can be a problem outside regular shopping hours.

Try to make the journey as much fun as the destination. Children love seeing points of interest, but they also adore riding ferries, rowing boats and taking trains.

● *Children having fun in the water and around the boats*

Sports & activities

Residents of the Neapolitan Riviera – just like Italians in general – love their sport. Whether playing or watching, locals are an active bunch thanks to both their passionate Mediterranean temperaments and the temperate weather they enjoy year round. While football rules the roost, there are plenty of other options if this does not appeal.

FOOTBALL

Neapolitans live and die by the fortunes of their resident football team SSC Napoli. All home matches for Napoli are played in the Stadio San Paolo, which is probably the most atmospheric stadium on match days in the entire country. Tickets sell out fast and you are advised to avoid the area at all costs on game days unless you are planning to attend, because the crowds can get both large and boisterous.

🄰 Stadio San Paolo, Piazzale Tecchio, Fuorigrotta 🄣 081 239 5623
🄛 Matches are played on alternate Sundays between Sept and June

HIKING

There are numerous hiking trails along the Neapolitan Riviera that may challenge you. Two of the more notable treks include up to the rim of the volcanic crater at Mount Vesuvius (see page 75) and the Trail of the Gods running along the Amalfi Coast from Positano to Praiano (see page 61). Of the two, the Trail of the Gods is the more challenging.

JOGGING & STROLLING

Neapolitans young and old enjoy nothing more than a stroll by the seafront or through a public park – the only difference is how fast you do it. Active types jog at dawn or during the day, while courting couples, families and elderly grannies take over the paths at dusk. There are no actual jogging tracks anywhere along the Neapolitan Riviera, and the narrow streets of the Amalfi Coast and islands in the bay make it almost impossible to navigate the ever-constant stream of cars. Instead, restrict your exertions to the promenade that lines Naples's seafront from Castel dell'Ovo to Mergellina or the parkland surrounding the Museo di Capodimonte.

SPAS

Ischia is the place to head if you are an avid spa-goer. The geothermally heated and mineral-rich waters have been attracting visitors for centuries due to their health-giving properties. For a list of spas, see page 33.

SWIMMING POOLS

If your hotel doesn't have a swimming pool and you are staying in Naples, avoid the decidedly murky city beaches and head to Collana, the city's only indoor swimming pool. The cost of admission includes access to the sundeck and deckchair rental. It may not be Capri, but it does the trick.

ⓐ Via Rossini, Naples ① 081 560 1988 ② 09.30–14.30, 15.30–21.00 Mon–Sat, 09.00–16.00 Sun July & Aug; closed Sept–June

🔺 *Relaxing in one of Ischia's thermal spas*

Festivals & events

January
La Befana Every year on 6 January, an old woman comes down from the sky and lands at the Piazza del Plebiscito to give gifts to the good children of Naples.

February/March
Carnevale Naples lets its hair down for this pre-Lenten party in February.
❶ 081 247 1123 ❶ The carnival dates can occur in March, depending on when Easter falls

March
Benvenuta Primavera For the month of March, homes and gardens usually restricted from public view are opened up for private tours and theatrical performances.
❶ 081 247 1123
Forio Easter processions are held in towns throughout the region.
❶ Dates vary according to when Easter falls

April
Settimana per la cultura For a single week in April, all the museums of Naples are opened to the masses free of charge.
Ⓦ www.beniculturali.it

May
Galassia Gutenburg Southern Italy's largest book fair.
❶ 081 320 3181 Ⓦ www.galassia.org (site in Italian only)
❶ Dates may vary
Maggio dei Monumenti The largest cultural festival in all of Naples, with public performances and events, many free of charge.
❶ 081 247 1123

San Costanzo Blessing of Capri's patron saint held every year on 14 May. Celebrations are held across all of Capri Town.

Villa San Michele Beginning of the summer concert season that runs until August.

ⓐ Villa San Michele in Anacapri

June

Estate a Napoli Plays, concerts and films performed under the stars in locations throughout the city of Naples all summer until September.

ⓣ 081 247 1123 ⓦ www.comune.napoli.it

Ischia Film Festival Started in 2003, this international film festival celebrates the brains behind film-making, rather than the actors and actresses. Directors, choreographers and the like receive recognition.

Sant'Andrea Three-day processional and fireworks display in Amalfi to honour the town's patron saint. Held every year 25–27 June.

Sant'Antonio di Padova Blessing of the patron saint of Anacapri and processional on 13 June. Join the festivals in Anacapri, where celebrations are planned throughout the town.

July

Feast of Saint Anne Torchlight procession and fireworks display held on 26 July in Ischia harbour.

Neapolis Festival International rock festival in Naples drawing big-name acts both foreign and domestic.

ⓦ www.neapolis.it

Santa Maria del Carmine Massive fireworks display held in Naples every year on 16 July to commemorate the destruction of the bell tower of the Santa Maria del Carmine church.

August

Ferragosto The feast of the Assumption is held on 15 August. The most interesting celebrations are in Positano.

September

Feast of San Gennaro The biggest bash of the lot – held to honour the patron saint of the city of Naples on 19 September.

Pizzafest Proud of their famously successful invention, the Neapolitans celebrate pizza! There are plenty of competitions, including dough-making contests. You can also taste the pizzas.
Ⓦ www.pizzafest.info

October

Salerno International Film Festival Small, yet well-selected, celebration of international film.
Ⓣ 089 231 953 Ⓦ www.festivaldelcinema.it

December

Capodanno Naples's Piazza del Plebiscito is the place to go along the coast when ringing in the New Year. Classical, rock and traditional musicians play to the crowds through the evening.

Natale Christmas celebrations last for a month leading up to Christmas Day. Every town brings out nativity scenes and churches programme concerts of sacred music.

▶ *Departures board at Stazione Circumvesuviana, Naples*

PRACTICAL INFORMATION
Tips & advice

PRACTICAL INFORMATION

Accommodation

Hotels in Italy are graded according to a star system running from one star for a cheap pensione to five stars for a luxurious resort with numerous facilities. The price guide below is based on the average price for a double room for two people:

£ = up to €100   **££** = €100–€200   **£££** = over €200

NAPLES

B & B Bellini £–££ Pristine and comfortable bed and breakfast in the leafy Piazza Bellini. A great location to be based for accessing many of the city's attractions. ⓐ Piazza Bellini 68 ⓣ 081 060 7338 ⓦ www.bbbellini.it

Britannique £–££ The favoured hotel for Europeans on a Grand Tour back in the 19th century. ⓐ Corso Vittorio Emanuele 133 ⓣ 081 761 4145 ⓦ www.hotelbritannique.it

Excelsior £££ The hotel of choice for visiting dignitaries. ⓐ Via Partenope 48 ⓣ 081 764 0111 ⓦ www.excelsior.it

PROCIDA

La Casa sul Mare ££ Restored 18th-century *palazzo* (palace) perfect for romancing couples. ⓐ Salita Castello 13 ⓣ 081 896 8799 ⓦ www.lacasasulmare.it ⓘ Closed 3 weeks in Jan & Feb

Hotel Ristorante Crescenzo ££ Small, family-run hotel right on the marina. ⓐ Via Marino di Chiaiolella 33 ⓣ 081 896 7255 ⓦ www.hotelcrescenzo.it

ISCHIA

Hotel La Marticana £–££ There are few hotels on Ischia that offer accommodation-only rates instead of half-board. This is one of the exceptions. ⓐ Via Quercia 48 ⓣ 081 993 230 ⓦ www.lamarticana.it

Miramare e Castello £££ Beachside location with spa packages available.
ⓐ Via Pontano 9 ⓣ 081 991 333 ⓦ www.miramareecastello.it
❗ Closed mid-Oct–mid-Apr

CAPRI
Villa Sarah ££ Intimate villa for those on a budget. ⓐ Via Tiberio 3A
ⓣ 081 837 7817 ⓦ www.villasarah.it ❗ Closed Nov–Mar

Villa Carmencita ££ Modern hotel with private garden in Anacapri.
ⓐ Viale T. de Tomasso 4 ⓣ 081 837 1360 ⓦ www.carmencitacapri.com
❗ Closed Nov–Mar

SORRENTO
Ostello delle Sirene (Youth Hostel) £ The cheapest beds in Sorrento –
if not the entire Sorrentine Peninsula. Dorm-style and private beds
available. ⓐ Via degli Aranci 160 ⓣ 081 807 2925

Grand Hotel Excelsior Vittoria £££ In operation since 1834, this hotel is
the grande dame of the city – considered by many to be the finest in
Campania. ⓐ Piazza Tasso 34 ⓣ 081 807 1044 ⓦ www.exvitt.it

Sorrentine Peninsula: north coast
Hotel Aequa ££ Romantic hotel in the heart of Vico Equense, with views
of Vesuvius. ⓐ Via Filangeri 46, Vico Equense ⓣ 081 801 5331

POSITANO
Hotel California ££ Family-run establishment with a beautiful flower-
strewn terrace. ⓐ Via Cristoforo Colombo 141 ⓣ 089 875 382
ⓦ www.hotelcaliforniapositano.it ❗ Closed Nov–Mar

PRAIANO
Hotel Le Sirene £–££ Simple hotel with views of the olive groves and a
rooftop solarium. ⓐ Via San Nicola 10 ⓣ 089 874 013
ⓦ www.lesirene.com ❗ Closed Nov–mid-Mar

Preparing to go

GETTING THERE
By air

The main entry point to the Neapolitan Riviera is Capodichino Airport, which is served by many major European airlines and some low-cost services. Travellers from the US or Canada will need to change planes at a European hub before reaching their final destination because there are no non-stop services.

Alitalia ☎ 0870 000 0123 Ⓦ www.alitalia.com
British Airways ☎ 0844 493 0787 Ⓦ www.ba.com
easyJet ☎ 0871 244 2366 Ⓦ www.easyjet.com
Fly Thomas Cook Ⓦ book.flythomascook.com

Many people are aware that air travel emits CO_2, which contributes to climate change. You may be interested in the possibility of lessening the environmental impact of your flight through the charity Climate Care, which offsets your CO_2 by funding environmental projects around the world. Visit Ⓦ www.jpmorganclimatecare.com

By rail

There are fast and comfortable connections using the Eurostar French routings from London's St Pancras International station. This involves a change in Paris and at Turin. You may also need to change trains at either Milan or Rome depending on which service you take. The total journey time is approximately 16–20 hours depending on connections. The monthly *Thomas Cook European Rail Timetable* has up-to-date schedules for European international and domestic train services.

Eurostar ☎ 08705 186 186 Ⓦ www.eurostar.com
Thomas Cook European Rail Timetable ☎ (UK) 01733 416 477
☎ (US) 1 800 322 3834 Ⓦ www.thomascookpublishing.com

By road

The Italian motorway system is well integrated into the European motorway network. The easiest motorway to use is the A1, which cuts through Italy and passes through Rome to terminate at Naples. The trip from London via Calais, Paris, Nice, Genoa, Florence and Rome may be picturesque but it's a long drive at approximately 20 hours.

If you happen to break down, national motoring groups (AA or RAC in the UK; the AAA/CAA in the US and Canada) have reciprocal agreements with the Automobile Club d'Italia (ACI):

ACI ⓐ Piazzale Tecchio 49D ⓣ 803 116 ⓦ www.aci.it

By bus

Long-distance buses connect Naples with most other European countries. Most travellers will have to change in Rome to reach their destination. The arrival point is outside the Stazione Centrale (Central Station). From London by National Express, the fastest journey time is about 24 hrs (ⓦ www.nationalexpress.com).

TOURISM AUTHORITY

Three local tourist boards serve the region. Each one provides maps and information of varying quality.

ASST ⓐ Via San Carlo 9, Naples ⓣ 081 402 394 ⓦ www.inaples.it
ⓛ 09.00–13.30, 15.00–19.30 Mon–Fri, 09.00–14.00 Sat & Sun
Ente Provinciale del Turismo (EPT) ⓐ Piazza dei Martiri ⓣ 081 410 721
ⓛ 09.00–14.00 Mon–Fri
Osservatorio Turistico-Culturale ⓐ Piazza del Plebiscito 14 ⓣ 081 247 1123
ⓦ www.comune.napoli.it ⓛ 09.00–19.00 Mon–Fri, 09.00–14.00 Sat
(and Sun certain periods, such as Easter or Christmas)
Another useful source of tourist information is **Italy Heaven**
ⓦ www.italyheaven.co.uk/campania

BEFORE YOU LEAVE
Health and prescriptions
Take regular prescription medicines with you to ensure that you don't
run out. Pack a small first-aid kit with plasters, antiseptic cream, travel
sickness pills, insect repellent and bite-relief creams, upset stomach
remedies, painkillers and protective suncreams. Consider a dental check
before you go if you are planning an extended stay in Italy. Ask your hotel
receptionist or your tour operator representative to recommend a doctor
or dentist in the event of an emergency.

Insurance
Check that your insurance policy covers you adequately for loss of
possessions and valuables, for activities you might want to try – say
horse riding or watersports – and for emergency medical and dental
treatment, including flights home, if required.

ENTRY FORMALITIES
Visitors to Italy who are citizens of the UK, Ireland, Australia, the
US, Canada or New Zealand will need a passport but not a visa for
stays of up to three months. After that time they must apply for a
permesso di soggiorno (permit to stay). If you are travelling from
other countries, you may need a visa and it is best to check before
you leave home.

MONEY
The currency in Italy is the euro. If you are coming from another country
in the European Union (EU) that uses euros, you will not need to change
money. You can withdraw money using ATMs (cash machines) at many
Italian banks.

The most widely accepted credit cards are Visa and MasterCard.
American Express is less commonly accepted.

CLIMATE

The Neapolitan Riviera experiences a Mediterranean climate, which means it is hot, dry and bright during the summer and cool and damp during the winter. The temperature rarely drops below 0°C (32°F); however, snow can be seen on Vesuvius during the winter months. Spring and autumn are considered the best times to visit when temperatures remain moderate, yet sunny.

BAGGAGE ALLOWANCE

Tightening of airline security has meant that baggage allowances are restricted for all passengers passing through the UK. Each passenger is allowed one item of cabin baggage through the airport search point measuring a maximum of 56 cm x 45 cm x 25 cm (22 x 18 x 10 inches). Handbags and other bags should be placed inside this one item.

It's better to place all liquid items, including water, other drinks, sprays, creams, pastes and gels, in your hold baggage if possible. If you really want to take liquids, gels and aerosols in your cabin baggage, you must place them in individual containers of 100 ml and carry them in a transparent, re-sealable bag no bigger than 20 cm x 20 cm (8 x 8 inches). For updates and more details on transport security, please see
Ⓦ www.dft.gov.uk

During your stay

AIRPORTS

Naples International Airport (Aeroporto Internazionale di Napoli
(Capodichino)) is 8 km (5 miles) away from the centre of Naples. While it
is southern Italy's largest airport, it isn't packed with facilities. Short-haul
traffic makes up the bulk of flights, with the occasional charter servicing
longer-haul destinations.

Getting to Naples from the airport is very easy. The journey to
Stazione Centrale railway station takes about 5 to 10 minutes, and
20 minutes to the ferry and hydrofoil ports. If you're on a budget, direct
bus services make the trip to both destinations throughout the day.
Alibus (❶ 800 639 525) is the most recommended private bus service,
departing every 30 minutes from outside the arrivals level of the airport
to the Piazza Garibaldi exit of the Stazione Centrale and Piazza
Municipio near the main port. Buses run from 05.55 to 23.55 daily and
cost €3 each way.

Local buses are also a possibility. Look for the orange route 3S bus,
which departs every 15 minutes from outside the arrivals lounge. Tickets
need to be purchased in advance from the tabaccherie (newsagents)
inside the airport and cost €1 each way. This method should only be
considered if you pack light as pickpockets are common. Don't forget to
stamp your ticket once you board.

Hailing a taxi isn't a problem as there are dozens waiting for each
and every passenger. Depending on traffic, the trip should cost between
€15 and €20.

COMMUNICATIONS
Telephones

Italian phone numbers need to be dialled with their area codes
regardless of where you are calling from. All numbers in Naples and its
province begin with 081. This includes Sorrento and the islands of Ischia,
Capri and Procida. Amalfi and Ravello, located in the province of Salerno,
have the code 089.

Phone numbers in Naples usually have seven digits. Older establishments may, however, have only six. All numbers beginning with 800 are toll-free. Mobile phone numbers always begin with 3.

Public phones tend to be placed at busy intersections. As a result, it can be a challenge hearing anything that is being said. The plus side is that almost everyone along the Riviera has a mobile so public phone booths are almost always available. The minimum charge for a local call is 10¢. You will need a phone card before you are permitted to make call. These are available from any of the numerous tabaccherie. Some phones may also take credit cards – usually at train stations and airports.

TELEPHONING ITALY

To call Italy from abroad, dial the codes listed below followed by the local number (including the code), but drop the first 0 from the Italian number. To call Naples, Capri, Ischia and Sorrento from within Italy dial 081 and then the number. Amalfi and the rest of the Amalfi coastline require a prefix dialled of 089. For operator assistance, call 170.

From the UK 0039
From the US & Canada 011 359
From Australia & New Zealand 00 11 359
From South Africa 090 359

TELEPHONING ABROAD

When making an international call from Italy, dial the international code you require and drop the initial zero of the area code you are ringing:

Australia 0061
Irish Republic 00353
New Zealand 0064
South Africa 0027
UK 0044
US & Canada 001

Mobile phone networks in Italy are: Wind, Vodafone, Tim, Tiscali and Infostrada. There are plenty of mobile phone shops. If you want an Italian SIM card, you will need to produce photo ID. The tabaccherie sell top-up cards.

Post

Italy's postal system is beginning to improve after decades of unreliability. Post boxes are red and have two slots divided between local destinations (*per la città*) and everywhere else (*tutte le altre destinazioni*). Some also have a section with a blue sticker on the front for first-class post.

For post being sent out of the country, first class is the only choice you have. First-class service promises 24-hour delivery for any destination in Italy, and three days for anywhere in the EU.

Letters less than 20 g posted within Italy or to other EU countries costs 65¢; to the US they cost 85¢. Australian post costs €1.20. Registered mail starts at €2.80.

Internet

Most Italian phone lines now have sockets for standard phone plugs (RJ11), although you'll need an adapter for the power supply. Broadband in hotels is still a bit of a luxury, unless you are staying in a major chain. And you might as well keep dreaming if you yearn for wireless services. Internet cafés are scattered throughout the city and surrounding areas – each one varying in speed. Try to choose a business centre in a hotel or a café with multiple terminals to ensure high-quality service.

CUSTOMS

English is not commonly spoken along the Neapolitan Riviera, so some advance preparation when trying to understand local customs is advised if you want to avoid offending residents.

The entire region is incredibly superstitious – especially the older generation. If someone explains that you shouldn't do something because it attracts the 'evil eye', then listen to them or they might think you are 'cursed'. Sundays are family day, so try not to make any plans with local friends unless it involves their inviting you to their weekly family gathering.

When talking, Neapolitans are very animated, using wild gesticulations – both when happy and sad. They may come up to you and invade your traditional sense of personal space, but this is not intended to threaten you (unless you happen to be in an argument). If you are having an argument, slowly back away, but if you back away during normal conversation, they may be offended.

Service in shops and restaurants is very slow. In shops, most items are folded away in drawers, and in restaurants, waiters may not approach you for quite a while. This is not meant to annoy you; rather, locals view eating and shopping as life's pleasures and they prefer to extend the time taken for them. For them, life is about quality rather than speed.

DRESS CODES

Shorts and T-shirts are absolutely fine when exploring the Neapolitan Riviera, until night falls. The entire region is extremely chic and a bumbag strapped over jogging trousers or a cotton T-shirt will immediately brand you as an uncouth tourist. For fine dining establishments (all day), or even when planning to check in to a five-star hotel, it is advisable to wear light cotton or linen suits (men) or summer dresses and blouses (women). Around the beaches, skimpy beachwear and topless bathing is common, but you would be frowned upon if you decided to walk through the streets of Naples in the same attire. On Capri or Positano, you can get away with beachwear on the streets – but only if you are wearing some sort of designer cover-up to protect your modesty!

On Sundays in any town, a more modest dress sense is advised in order to respect religious sensibilities.

ELECTRICITY

The standard electrical current is 220 volts (50 Hertz). Two-pin adapters can be purchased at most electrical shops.

EMERGENCY NUMBERS
Ambulance 118
Car breakdown 803 116
Carabinieri (national/military police) 112
Fire brigade 115
Polizia di Stato (national police) 113

GETTING AROUND
Public transport

Naples used to be difficult to get around by public transport. Now that the metro system is up and running, this is no longer such a problem. While the lines won't take you everywhere you want to go, they cover a lot of ground in the city centre. Bus routes are more extensive, but the traffic often means it takes longer to get to your destination by bus than by walking. A dedicated bus lane along the Corso Umberto between San Carlo and the Stazione Centrale (Central Station) does help matters if you are trying to make a beeline for the port and Royal Naples.

Bus tickets must be purchased in advance from any *tabaccheria* (newsagent) for €1.10 each. Once you board, don't forget to get the ticket stamped. The ticket is valid for 90 minutes. Metro and funicular tickets also cost €1.10 each, but can be purchased at the station.

For travel along the coast and onwards to Sorrento, the Circumvesuviana train line is the best option. Trains depart frequently from Naples's Stazione Circumvesuviana, making stops at Herculaneum, Pompeii and Vico Equense along the way. The complete journey takes approximately one hour. Information about fares and schedules can be obtained at ⓦ www.vesuviana.it (Italian only) or by calling toll-free on ❶ 800 053 939.

Ferries to Sorrento, Amalfi, Salerno, Capri, Procida and Ischia depart from the Terminal Aliscafi at Mergellina. There are a number of operators that ply the routes so chances are a ferry of some kind should be departing within the hour of your arrival at the port. Fast services by hydrofoil only run during the high summer season.

Ferry services also run directly to the islands from the Amalfi Coast, but these departures are much less frequent than the port at Sorrento, which offers the most options. Inter-island transport is also available.

Once on the Amalfi Coast, coach services are the way to travel in order to reach resorts such as Positano and Praiano. Be aware that coach services are extremely limited on Sundays – especially during the winter season. On public holidays and between November and March, weekends may see complete cancellations of scheduled pick-ups. If you have a fear of heights in any way, stay away from the window seats as the Amalfi Coast road was originally intended for horses and carriages, not coaches or trucks. This advice is key when two coaches attempt to pass each other along the journey (which happens a lot more frequently than you might like).

🔺 You can't miss the distinctive red metro signs

Car hire

Unless you are planning an Amalfi Coast drive, don't hire a car – it won't get you anywhere fast, you won't find anywhere to park it, and you'll most likely get it scratched. For fast access within Naples, consider renting a scooter. Car rental on the islands is ill-advised, with Ischia being the only resort where having a car may sometimes come in handy.

The minimum age for renting an economy car is 21. For a larger car you need to be 25. Most rental companies require you to be covered for both theft and collision-damage insurance, but even if they don't, then get it anyway. Most companies have sat nav devices to rent.

Local and international rental companies include:

Avis ☎ 199 100 133 🔵 www.avis.com
Budget ☎ 848 867 067 🔵 www.budget.co.uk
Europcar ☎ 800 014 410 🔵 www.europcar.com
Hertz ☎ 081 780 2971 🔵 www.hertz.com
Thrifty ☎ 081 780 5702 🔵 www.italybycar.it

HEALTH, SAFETY & CRIME

It is not necessary to take any special health precautions while travelling in Italy. Tap water is safe to drink, but do not drink any water from lakes or rivers as the region is not known for its commitment towards environmentalism. Many Italians prefer bottled mineral water, especially sparkling varieties.

As the region is quite arid and hilly, hiking is a popular pastime. If you do decide to go for a stroll, it is best to inform someone before you set off on your journey as conditions can change fast – especially at the top of Vesuvius. Be aware that signs will be posted on days when a climb up Vesuvius is not permitted. Do not ignore these warnings as they may be related to seismic activity that could make you ill, if not kill you. Heatstroke is also a common problem so don't go anywhere without appropriate clothing and ample water supplies. Many visitors experience heatstroke when exploring Pompeii due to the lack of shade, so a hat and plenty of sunscreen are vital.

Pharmacies (*farmacie*) are marked by a large green or red cross. Italian pharmacists can provide informal medical advice on simple ailments, but prescriptions will always cost more to fill than they do back home.

Italian healthcare is of a good standard, but it is not free. In most cases your travel insurance should provide the cover you need, but remember to bring your EHIC (the old E111 form, available at post offices or from Ⓦ www.dh.gov.uk) for reduced-cost treatment.

Crime has always been a problem in the city of Naples and along the coast. Its reputation is far worse than the reality. Petty theft (bag-snatching, pickpocketing) is the most common form of trouble for tourists and activity is particularly high in the much-frequented historic sights and near the train stations and ferry ports. You are unlikely to experience violence or assault, which occur mainly in the context of gangland activities. Don't carry too much cash and try not to walk around late at night on badly lit streets (especially if you are a woman). Your hotel will warn you about particular areas to avoid.

When using public transport or walking on the street, carry your wallet in your front pocket, keep bags closed at all times, never leave valuables on the ground when you are seated at a table, and always wear camera bags and purses crossed over your chest.

MEDIA
Newspapers

Italian news is a very local affair, with headlines focusing on what's happening closer to home rather than nationally or internationally. The major daily for the region is *Il Mattino*, but *La Repubblica* from Rome and Milan's *Corriere della Sera* have sections covering Naples and Campania. All these publications are written in Italian only.

Tabloid publications covering human interest, sport and sensationalism are also popular. It is not uncommon for any Neapolitan to pick up a broadsheet for the news coverage and a sport daily for their dose of football fixtures and updates.

For international publications, head to a newsstand – specifically in Naples. Kiosks in Naples will receive British newspapers and the *International Herald Tribune* either the same day or a day after publication in the UK. Kiosks along the Amalfi Coast and on the outlying islands may have a longer delay, so if you are on your way to either destination, pick up your valued reads before leaving the port or train station. Magazines are readily available and tend to be either very news-orientated (*The Economist*, *Time*) or high on fashion and celebrity (*Vogue*, *OK!*, *Heat*).

Television
There are six networks – three state-owned and three owned by the Prime Minister Silvio Berlusconi. If staying at a hotel with satellite or cable, you will have access to two English-language stations – BBC World and CNN.

Radio
Three state-owned stations – similar in output to the BBC stations of the UK – play easy-listening, jazz and classical music, and provide regular news updates. For more popular hits and UK/US chart options, tune in to either Rock Capital (88.05 or 104.75 FM) or Rock Kiss Kiss (99.25 or 103.0 FM). Rock Kiss Kiss also broadcasts the matches of SSC Napoli live on game days. Alternatively, tune in to American Forces Radio on 106.0 if you want a slice of North America during your southern Italian stay.

OPENING HOURS
Most businesses open 09.00–18.00 Monday–Friday. Retail shops stay open until 20.00 with a two- to three-hour lunch break starting around 13.30. Restaurants and cafés usually close between lunch and dinner from 15.30 until 19.00. Most also remain closed for breakfast. Many companies close for large parts of the month of August – except on the Amalfi Coast and on the islands of Capri, Ischia and Procida when the season is in full swing. Banks open 08.20–13.20 & 14.45–15.45 Monday–Friday.

Cultural institutions normally close for one day per week – usually Monday or Tuesday. Only the biggest and most popular sights remain open seven days a week. Sundays will, however, have limited hours. Usual post office opening hours are 08.15–19.00 Monday–Friday and 08.15–12.00 Saturday.

RELIGION

While Italians are not extremely religious and going to mass is becoming a less-frequent ritual for the younger generation, Naples and the entire Riviera remains fiercely Roman Catholic. This is especially true around the feast days of the various patron saints of the resort communities. Sundays remain an important family day with many businesses shutting up shop – even during the height of the season.

TIME DIFFERENCES

Italian clocks follow Central European Time (CET). During Daylight Saving Time (end Mar–end Oct), the clocks are put ahead one hour. In the Italian summer, at 12.00 noon, time back home is as follows:

Australia Eastern Standard Time 20.00, Central Standard Time 19.30, Western Standard Time 18.00
New Zealand 22.00
South Africa 12.00
UK and Republic of Ireland 11.00
US and Canada Newfoundland Time 07.30, Atlantic Canada Time 07.00, Eastern Standard Time 06.00, Central Time 05.00, Mountain Time 04.00, Pacific Time 03.00, Alaska 02.00

TIPPING

Tipping is not obligatory along the Riviera, with the exception of some of the better restaurants where 10 per cent is expected. If a service charge is included on your receipt, you will not be expected to add any more on top. Chambermaids and porters should be given about €1 a day, while taxi drivers will appreciate it if you round your fare up to the nearest euro.

TOILETS

There are very few public toilet facilities along the Neapolitan Riviera. The best approach is to use the toilet in a bar. You can usually walk straight in without having to buy a drink. If the bar is empty, it is a matter of politeness to ask the bartender first. In restaurants there may be signs saying that toilets are only for use by paying customers. The facilities in fast-food joints and department stores are also good options.

TRAVELLERS WITH DISABILITIES

For people with disabilities, the Neapolitan Riviera is notoriously difficult to negotiate. The best thing to do is to ask someone who works at the location you want to enter if they can help you, as there may be ramps that can be placed over stairs. In museums the ground floors are usually accessible, as are those in more modern galleries. Buses, however, are completely wheelchair unfriendly. If you need to get around, try using the modern and efficient metro and overground trains instead. New metro stations in Naples have wheelchair access features (ramps and lifts) incorporated into the design. Yet, even where ramps exist, you will often find them obstructed by cars or motorcycles.

The historic sights of Pompeii and Herculaneum, while outdoors, are little better. Access to the actual collection of ruins may have ramps, but the pathways date back to the original Roman period and are littered with wheel ruts and cracks making manoeuvring difficult.

Ⓦ www.sath.org (US-based site)

Ⓦ www.access-able.com (general advice on worldwide travel)

A

Abbazia di San Michele Arcangelo 24
accommodation 108–9
air travel 110, 113, 114
Amalfi 82–4, 98
Anacapri 35
ATMs 112

B

baggage allowance 113
Baia di San Montano 30
banks 122
beaches 99
    see also individual locations
Blue Grotto 36, 37
boat trips 11, 24, 36, 57, 59
buses, city 118
buses, long-distance 111, 119

C

Calcare 50
Campanian Minerals Museum 54
Capodimonte Museum 16
Capri 9, 10, 34–41, 95, 109
car hire 120
castles 15, 16, 24, 30
Certosa di San Giacomo 37
children 99–101
churches 45, 53, 64
climate and seasons 113
Conca dei Marini 63
credit cards 96, 112
crime 96, 121
currency 112
customs, local 116–17

D

disabilities, travellers with 124
dress codes 91, 117
drinking water 120
driving 111, 120

E

eating out 88–94, 122
    see also individual locations
Eco-Museum 65
Edenlandia 99
electricity 117
Emerald Grotto 63, 65
emergencies 118

F

ferry services 118–19
festivals and events 104–6
flea market 96
food and drink 88–94
football 10, 102
Fornillo 59

H

health 112, 120–1
Herculaneum 74, 75, 77, 96, 124
home security 112
hotels 108–9

I

insurance 112, 121
Internet access 116
Ischia 9, 28–33, 103, 108–9

L

La Mortella 32
language 92–4
Li Galli 57
limoncello 10, 36, 89–90, 96–7

M

Marina de Equa 50
Marina di Furore 63
Marina di Praia 63
Marina di Vico 50
markets 96, 98
medical treatment 112, 121
menu decoder 92–4
Meta di Sorrento 50

money 112, 123
Mount Solaro 37–8
Mount Vesuvius 10, 74–7, 78, 79, 102, 113, 120
museums 18, 39, 45, 47, 52, 53, 65, 70, 82, 86, 100

N
Naples 9, 11, 14–21, 95, 96, 99, 103, 108, 118, 121
newspapers 121–2
nightlife *see* individual locations

O
opening hours 122–3
opera 11, 18

P
Paper Museum 82
passports and visas 100, 112
Pezzolo 50
pharmacies 121
pizza 11, 91, 106
police 118
Pompeii 10, 74, 78–81, 100, 120, 124
Positano 56–62, 95, 98, 109
postal services 116, 123
Pozzo Vecchio 22
Praiano 63–6, 109
Procida 9, 22–7, 108
public transport 118–19
Punta Caruso 30

R
radio 122
religion 123
Rome 68–73

S
Salerno 85–6
Sant'Agnello 50
scuba diving 59, 64
shopping 11, 95–8, 117, 122

Sorrentine Peninsula 50–5
Sorrento 9, 42–9, 95, 98, 109
souvenirs 96, 98
spas 9, 33, 103
Spiaggia di Alimuri 52
sports and activities 11, 102–3
sun safety 120
swimming pools 103

T
Teatro di San Carlo 11, 18
telephones 114–16
television 122
time differences 123
tipping 123
toilets 124
Torre del Greco 77
tourist information 111
Trail of the Gods 61, 102
train services 110, 118

V
Vatican City 71
Vettica Maggiore 63, 64
Vico Equense 50
Villa Damecuta 39
Villa Jovis 39
Villa San Michele 39

W
walking and hiking 52, 61, 75, 102, 120
wines and liqueurs 10, 88–90, 96, 98

Y
youth hostel 109

ACKNOWLEDGEMENTS

We would like to thank the following for providing their copyright photographs for this book: Francesco Allegretto pages 17, 31, 54, 76; BigStockPhoto.com/Danilo Ascione page 46; Dreamstime.com/David Iliff page 70; Getty Images/Dallas Stribley page 21; Roy Rainford page 42; Travel Inkpage 8; Guido Alberto Rossi/Tips Images page 87; Mark Bassett pages 5, 10–11, 13, 23, 25, 29, 35, 38, 49, 58, 60, 64, 67, 78, 80, 83, 88, 97, 98, 101, 103, 107, 119; cuboimages/Photoshot page 51; Pictures Colour Library pages 1, 73; Wikimedia Commons page 74.

Project editor: Catherine Burch
Layout: Trevor Double
Proofreader: Nick Newton
Indexer: Marie Lorimer

Send your thoughts to
books@thomascook.com

- Found a beach bar, peaceful stretch of sand or must-see sight that we don't feature?

- Like to tip us off about any information that needs a little updating?

- Want to tell us what you love about this handy little guidebook and more importantly how we can make it even handier?

Then here's your chance to tell all! Send us ideas, discoveries and recommendations today and then look out for your valuable input in the next edition of this title.

Email to the above address or write to:
pocket guides Series Editor, Thomas Cook Publishing, PO Box 227, Coningsby Road, Peterborough PE3 8SB, UK.

Useful phrases

English	Italian	Approx pronunciation

BASICS		
Yes	Sì	*See*
No	No	*Noh*
Please	Per favore	*Pehr fahvohreh*
Thank you	Grazie	*Grahtsyeh*
Hello	Buongiorno/Ciao	*Bwonjohrnoh/Chow*
Goodbye	Arrivederci/Ciao	*Ahreevehderchee/Chow*
Excuse me	Scusi	*Skoozee*
Sorry	Mi dispiace	*Mee deespyahcheh*
That's okay	Va bene	*Vah behneh*
I don't speak Italian	Non parlo italiano	*Non pahrloh eetahlyahnoh*
Do you speak English?	Parla inglese?	*Pahrlah eenglehzeh?*
Good morning	Buongiorno	*Bwonjohrnoh*
Good afternoon	Buon pomeriggio	*Bwon pohmehreejoh*
Good evening	Buona sera	*Bwonah sehrah*
Goodnight	Buona notte	*Bwonah nohteh*
My name is ...	Mi chiamo ...	*Mee kyahmoh ...*

NUMBERS		
One	Uno	*Oonoh*
Two	Due	*Dooeh*
Three	Tre	*Treh*
Four	Quattro	*Kwahttroh*
Five	Cinque	*Cheenkweh*
Six	Sei	*Say*
Seven	Sette	*Sehteh*
Eight	Otto	*Ohtoh*
Nine	Nove	*Nohveh*
Ten	Dieci	*Dyehchee*
Twenty	Venti	*Ventee*
Fifty	Cinquanta	*Cheenkwahntah*
One hundred	Cento	*Chentoh*

SIGNS & NOTICES		
Airport	Aeroporto	*Ahehrohpohrtoh*
Railway station	Stazione ferroviaria	*Statsyoneh fehrohveeahreeyah*
Platform	Binario	*Beenahreeyoh*
Smoking/non-smoking	Fumatori/non fumatori	*Foomahtohree/non foomahtohree*
Toilets	Bagni	*Bahnyee*
Ladies/Gentlemen	Signore/Signori	*Seenyoreh/Seenyohree*
Subway	Metropolitana	*Mehtrohpohleetahnah*